THE ULTIMATE
VENISON
COOKBOOK

Jim & Ann Casada

Published by

 **krause publications**
An imprint of F+W Publications, Inc.

700 East State Street • Iola, WI 54990-0001
715-445-2214 • 888-457-2873
www.krause.com
Our toll-free number to place an order or obtain
a free catalog is (800) 258-0929.

Library of Congress Catalog Number: 2004093860

ISBN: 0-87349-744-9

Designed by Patsy Howell
Edited by Joel Marvin

Printed in the United States of America

Table of Contents

Fancy Fixings *(cont.)*

6

Chapter 6
Unusual Approaches: Sausage, Organ Meats,

Unusual Approaches: Sausage, Organ Meats, Jerky and More *(cont.)*

Chapter 7
Venison Through the Year: Cooking for All Seasons **186**

Appendix

Acknowledgments

Any work of this magnitude finds the authors incurring numerous debts of gratitude. For both of us, our foremost debt is to our parents. They ate little venison, not because it was unwelcome on the family table but because it was unavailable. Game figured regularly in the family diet, but we grew up in a time (the 1950s) and in places (western North Carolina and southside Virginia) where deer were extremely scarce. Yet our parents fully appreciated the bounty of the good earth, lived close to the land and imbued us with a connectedness to the natural world that included eating wild game. We relish memories of those simpler days and simpler ways and revere those who made them possible.

We owe thanks to those folks at Krause, most notably Don Gulbrandsen and Joel Marvin, who have been involved in shepherding this work along the sometimes rocky road to published reality. Also, it has and continues to be a pleasure to work with editors at Krause who are both real professionals and fine friends—Brian Lovett, Dan Schmidt and Jim Schlender.

It will come as no real surprise to anyone who hunts that the close-knit if widespread family of those who communicate the outdoor experience are exceptionally fine folks. Over the years we have come to know many of them well through membership in the South Carolina Outdoor Press Association, the Southeastern Outdoor Press Association and the Outdoor Writers Association of America. These folks are an ongoing inspiration to us as well as gracious almost to a fault in helping with projects such as this.

A number of friends made special contributions through sharing recipes or tips. We appreciate the help of Betty Robinson, Gail Wright, Jim Heine, Doug and Martha Smith, Larry Chesney, Eric Volner, Ted and Kaye Upgren, and Virginia Whedon in this regard. An especially heartfelt thank you goes to my good hunting buddy, Roy Turner, and his wife, Kerry. They generously shared some surplus venison with us at a time when the need to test recipes had outstripped the contents of our freezers.

Finally, we appreciate the input of our daughter, Natasha, and her husband, Eric, even as we eagerly anticipate the day when our granddaughter, Ashyln, can join her "Papooh" in sharing a deer stand.

Introduction

Our earlier cookbook, *The Complete Venison Cookbook,* has been in print for almost a decade. The fact that we have returned to the same publisher provides ample indication that we have been pleased with its sales, and presumably Krause's contracting with us for the present work shows similar satisfaction on their part. Our primary regret is a simple one – the choice of a title for the first venison cookbook.

It seemed appropriate at the time, given the fact that we endeavored to cover all aspects of venison cookery, and in the sense that we addressed all edible parts of the animal there was some completeness. Evidently another author was thinking along similar lines, because within a year there was another cookbook on the market with precisely the same title. That miffed us at the time, since it seemed inappropriate at best, but on reflection it may well be possible that the author had not researched other venison cookbooks and was unaware of another book with that title.

In a wider context, we should have realized that no cookbook can be truly "complete." That's the beauty of the culinary arts, whether they deal with venison or other foodstuffs. The only limit to venison recipes and use of the wonderful animal that is the whitetail comes with the energy and ingenuity of the cook. We've discovered as much in the years since the publication of this work's predecessor, and here's the result.

At this juncture we don't know whether we will ever write another cookbook, but should that be the case, rest assured that the word "complete" won't figure in the title. One of our favorite quotations from matters connected with the wild world comes from the man often described as the "Dean of American Campers," Horace Kephart. The author of, among other books, *Camp Cookery* and *Camping and Woodcraft,* Kephart rightly suggested that "in the school of the woods there is no graduation day." As someone who loved to cook and who turned out delicious meals with the simplest of tools used over a campfire, Kephart would certainly have also agreed that in the school of game cookery there is no graduation day. Rather, when one deals with venison cookery, he embarks on an ongoing voyage of discovery. Not all discoveries will delight the palate and lift the spirits (in writing this cookbook we tried a few things that just didn't work, and they have been duly relegated to the scrap heap of culinary failures), but most will.

In the chapters that follow you will find close to 200 recipes – none of which appeared in our previous venison cookbook – that span the entire spectrum of venison cookery. We are simple folks, and in large

measure these recipes reflect that fact. By the same token though, we prefer to venture well beyond the bounds of what Ann likes to refer to as "stomach stuffers."That means that while many of the recipes here are simple in terms of preparation, they nonetheless offer fair promise of proving gourmet fare.

We have given considerable thought to health-related issues. That is reflected throughout in recipe ingredients, and one chapter has been devoted exclusively to "health-smart" venison. In truth though, when compared with beef or indeed any type of domestic meat, venison has many special virtues. Before turning to those, however, mention should be made of the fact that venison can carry toxoplasmosis. For most of us, that is not a matter for particular concern, but for any woman who is pregnant or is hoping to conceive, awareness of this disease and the dangers it can pose for an unborn fetus is essential. Otherwise, though, from a health perspective, venison consumption makes a great deal of sense. It has never known the inoculants, vitamin supplements, growth hormones, questionable feeding practices and crowded conditions endemic to the beef industry. Instead, it promises much less fat (and what there is should be removed insofar as possible when the animal is processed), lower levels of cholesterol and top-level nutritional value. The American Heart Association has endorsed venison as a heart healthy red meat, and when properly handled, processed, and prepared, it tastes every bit as good as the finest cuts of beef – but delightfully different.

Speaking of handling and processing, those who are interested in details will want to pay careful heed to the first chapter of this book, "Readying Your Deer." Doing so will remove the problematic aspects of dealing with the recipes provided in the ensuing chapters. Most folks have at least part of their processing done commercially, and certainly this is convenient although not necessarily the best way to get things done. You have little or no control over how the meat is handled, how long it is aged, cleanliness and the like. If you have the time, tools and facilities to "do your own," there's certainly a staunch argument to be made for taking this route. If you do so, a book you might want to read is John Weiss' *Butchering Deer* (2002).

Even if you leave the processing and packaging to others, there are a number of steps you can take to ensure the best in venison. These include:

*Make clean, killing shots. One that drops the deer in its tracks is ideal, while a wounded animal that runs a long way seems to generate fluids that affect taste.

*Field dress the deer at once. The sooner you can get the body cavity open and the cooling process started, the better. For those who utilize the organ meats, and we recommend that you do so, carrying

along heavy-duty Ziploc bags for storage is recommended. Also, when it comes to field dressing, be prepared to take care of things in advance. That means having a good, sharp knife, ideally equipped with a gut hook, along with disposable gloves with long sleeves of the type offered by Hunters Specialties.

*Keep in mind that you don't need a trophy buck for gourmet fare. In fact, your best bet is to take mature does. They will offer ample amounts of meat, and in almost all areas of the country, you are also doing your part to keep buck-to-doe ratios more evenly balanced. Of course, even a venerable old mossyhorn can be turned into fine dishes – it just requires more aging and some consideration of what cuts to use.

*Speaking of aging, that aspect of getting venison ready ranks right alongside prompt field dressing in terms of importance. Hanging, preferably for periods of seven to 10 days, greatly improves venison. Better still (though you can seldom do this with commercial processors), hang the animal with the hide intact. If you don't have the opportunity to hang an animal for aging, you can do a reasonable job by quartering it and utilizing big coolers with ice in the bottom to do the job. Just make sure to keep the meat suspended above the ice.

*Take great care in removing fat, silver skin, scent glands and blood-tainted meat at entry and exit wounds. Similarly, exercise every care when it comes to cleanliness.

*Whether you package your own meat or have it done for you, good wrapping is a must. Vacuum sealing is recommended, or at least use butcher's paper and package the individual cuts with care. In the case of sausage, ground meat or other situations where fat or other ingredients are added, use only the best.

*Take care in labeling individual packages before they go into the freezer. That way there's no doubt about what the package holds. Also, dating the packages will give the indication you need about which ones should be used first. Generally speaking, a year is about as long as you should keep venison in the freezer, although when it is packaged in a manner that avoids any build-up of ice crystals and risk of freezer burn, it will last longer. A good general plan is to clean out and use any meat left over from the previous year just prior to the onset of a new hunting season.

All of these pointers are covered in considerably greater detail in Chapter 1, but they are so essential that a touch of redundancy is merited. Beyond that, Chapters 2 through 7 get down to the essentials. That is to say, recipes on how to use venison handled and processed along the lines recommended in the opening chapter.

We live in a health-conscious world, one where all sorts of diets and dietary supplements, along with seemingly endless concerns about

becoming a nation of couch potatoes and the wasteland of waists, assault us in advertisements and through the media at every turn. Without getting into the pros and cons of fads such as the Atkins diet, suffice it to say that for those interested in low-carbohydrate approaches, venison has a great deal to offer. The same holds true for many other aspects of health awareness, and Chapter 2, "Health Smart," recognizes this fact. Of course, it should be noted that the health benefits of venison are by no means limited exclusively to this chapter. It is better for you than beef – period. And if this gets us in trouble with farmers, well, that's just the way things will have to be.

While we are, as has already been suggested, pretty simple folks who enjoy a simple lifestyle and have neither the inclination (nor the financial wherewithal) to dine in five-star establishments on a regular basis, that doesn't mean we don't like what Jim's grandfather loved to describe as "fancy fixin's." Chapter 3 looks at venison in this context, and if you want to do something really memorable for visitors or on special occasions, you will find a bevy of recipes here that fit the bill.

In Chapter 4, we turn from food that is festive and fancy to equally flavorful but less complex recipes featuring ground venison. In truth, this is our favorite way to eat venison. Other than backstraps and tenderloins, we regularly have most of our deer ground up. From meatballs to shepherd's pies, from Tex-Mex dishes to ethnic ones we associate with Italy or Greece, ground venison can provide meals that are, as the title of this chapter suggests, "Simple and Scrumptious."

As these words are being written, we can look out the window at what the gurus of weather (yeah, I know, that may be an oxymoron) have termed the snow of a century. Four days ago, the Carolina skies dumped almost two feet of snow on the countryside where we live, and as it fell, some sort of innate gustatory response seemed to be triggered. We had a hankering for hearty foods. In our household, that means soups and stews, and in Chapter 5 that's what you get. Such recipes seem especially well suited for days when the chill bites to the bone and when the ravages of cabin fever threaten to reach epidemic levels. However, they also lend themselves to camp meals, clean-out-the-freezer gatherings where you entertain hunting buddies or fellow club members and situations where you want to put some food away that can be warmed up when a meal in a hurry is needed.

Far too often we, as hunters, fail to utilize our kills in the complete fashion that sound sporting ethics demands. When you study the way that the Inuit in portions of Canada used caribou, for example (read Farley Mowat's *People of the Deer* if this intrigues you), we fail abysmally. While turning hides into clothing, bones into bows and sinew into string may take matters further than most of us want to go, that

doesn't mean we shouldn't turn all edible parts of the animals we take into food. Doing so seems to be far too unusual, hence the title of Chapter 6, "Unusual Approaches: Sausage, Organ Meats, Jerky and More." It is not likely that every recipe here will be to your taste or suit your dining inclinations, but before you dismiss dining on heart or stuffing skins full of savory sausage, give them a careful look.

Finally, venison should be considered a meat for all seasons, and the concluding chapter looks at it in that fashion. The title of Chapter 7, "Venison Through the Year: Cooking for All Seasons," pretty well sums up our thoughts on the matter. We eat and enjoy deer meat throughout the year, and to make it easier for you to do the same, we travel the extra mile, so to speak, in this chapter. To make matters even easier, the chapter concludes with a dozen full menus - all of them containing one or more recipes from this cookbook - that will give you a map for wonderful meals for all seasons and every reason.

Throw in an appendix offering some information on contacts you might find useful when it comes to obtaining spices, processing equipment, helpful cutlery and the like, and there you have it. About all that remains is to wish you *bon appétit* and usher you into the pages that follow in fond hopes they will bring you an ample measure of dining pleasure.

Chapter 1

Readying Your Deer for the Table

Enjoying venison at its finest begins the moment you squeeze the trigger and continues through field dressing, cleaning, aging, processing, packaging and, ultimately, cooking. Indeed, in a certain sense, premium venison and readying the meat for the table begins even before you take a shot and experience the bittersweet moment inevitably associated with standing over a noble animal you have just killed.

Shots as They Relate to Fine Venison

The finest meat will come from a deer that is shot cleanly and dies quickly. That means paying your marksmanship dues in terms of spending the necessary time at a shooter's bench or shooting range to make sure your gun or bow afford optimal performance. Those same sessions also provide the hunter intimate familiarity with his weapon of choice and the element of self-confidence that looms so large in effective shot placement.

The details of marksmanship belong in technical training manuals, not a cookbook, but a few general thoughts on shooting a deer as they relate to venison do seem to be in order. In areas where deer abound, limits are liberal and the seasons long, the ideal approach is to take a suitable number of does for the freezer. As a welcome by-product to such hunting, you make a small but significant contribution to quality deer management through helping maintain a sound buck-to-doe ratio. If you feel sufficiently confident in your shooting ability and the situation permits it, try to take mature does and shoot them in the head or neck. Such shots do two meaningful things when it comes to enjoying the products of your hunt. First, they mean a quick death, something that is infinitely preferable to a poor shot that leaves the animal wounded and perhaps involves a long tracking process and stress that negatively affects the meat. Secondly, you have minimal or no waste of venison.

Once the Deer Is Down

Once your deer is down, no matter your shot placement, the time to get busy is at hand. At best, you have roughly two hours to remove the entrails before serious deterioration in the quality of the venison begins. In warm weather or with gut shot animals, that time becomes much shorter. Unless some pressing consideration such as means of disposing of the entrails prevents it, you should field dress your deer immediately. In truth, you can anticipate this by carrying some heavy-duty garbage bags in your daypack or small backpack to handle entrails. Double- or triple-bag the offal, and you can then transport it to a suitable place for proper disposal.

When field dressing the animal, following a few basic steps makes the process a simple, straightforward one. Get the deer on its back where the ground is smooth and fairly level, trying, if the terrain permits, to get the head elevated a bit. This lets the entrails settle into the body cavity and makes the cut to open the deer a bit easier. Once the deer is in place, it is a good idea to put on a pair of plastic or rubber gloves (Hunters Specialties makes disposable ones perfect for the task) for the work that lies before you. Although many folks open a deer by starting at the rear, a preferred approach is to begin at the point where the ribs come together. You can get started here without fear of going too deep and penetrating the stomach (something to be avoided at all costs).

After making a small slit of two to three inches, the only way to open a deer is by cutting up (away from the entrails). A knife with a gut hook has the functional design to do this, but you can perform the function with any sharp, sturdy knife. Insert your fingers through the slit and then slip the knife between them. Use your fingers to hold the skin lifted and taut and ease the knife along, cutting upward from the body cavity. By doing this, you avoid the chance of getting into the stomach. You also keep from cutting hair – something that dulls the knife's edge – and getting it on the meat.

Once the body cavity has been opened from the rib cage to the genital area, remove the genitals from a buck (in some states, you must leave these attached until the animal has been checked in or reported to wildlife authorities). Next, cut the hide in a complete circle around the deer's anal area, including the vagina when dressing a doe. This should extend inward underneath the arch of the pelvic bone. Work carefully, because you want to avoid cutting into the bladder or slicing the end of the intestine. Then tie off the intestine with a piece of string (or have a buddy pinch it if you have any help). This keeps "deer berries" where they belong as you ease the material away from the anal area. When everything is clear, cut the intestine just below where it has been tied off.

Now you are ready to remove the guts. Complete the cut all the way to the anal opening, and then straddle the body of the deer or one of the hindquarters if it is a large animal. From the back of the deer reach underneath the entrails, working underneath the bladder, and pull everything toward the front where you began your original cut. As everything pulls loose, tip to the side a bit and allow the stomach to tip over the open flank. Once that is clear, you can cut the stomach and entrails away from the esophagus. Now you have everything in the deer's upper body to remove.

If you belong to the company of those who enjoy organ meats – and when you eat them, there is at least the knowledge that they come from an animal that has eaten nothing but a natural diet – this is the time to set them aside. Both deer liver and heart are delicious, and you can also utilize the kidneys, which will still be attached along each side of the back, if desired. In the case of the liver, which is located tight against the diaphragm that separates the upper interior from the stomach, be sure not to confuse it with the much smaller spleen. The spleen looks a bit like a miniature liver and is somewhat grayish in color as opposed to the bright red of the liver. Unlike the rest of the edible

portions of a whitetail, organ meats do not need any aging. The ideal approach is to carry a few large, strong Ziploc bags with you for storing organ meats. An alternative is to use muslin bags to carry the organs. They soak up most of the extra blood or moisture that invariably drains off after you separate the organs. Cut them away and place in these bags. Once the field dressing process has been completed and you have gotten your deer to a processor or hanging in a cooler, you can return to the organ meats. Just wash them clean and freeze, or, if you plan to eat the meat in the next three or four days, put them in a cooler on ice or in a refrigerator.

Complete the removal of the lungs and esophagus and tilt the carcass, as necessary, to allow any blood to flow free. If you have killed the deer with a shot through the lungs or heart, you may also want to try to wipe away the offal left from the bullet's passage. Should yours be the misfortune to have made a gut shot, that needs to be cleaned up as much as possible in the field-dressing process. One way to do this is with a bunch of paper towels (pieces of these can do double duty as markers when you have to track a wounded animal), or an old, clean towel can be carried along for wiping everything up. You are now ready to get the deer to a cooler or, in colder climates, to hang it in a suitable place for aging. If the weather is particularly warm, cut a stick or two and use them to keep the body cavity open. This lets air circulate and enables the carcass to cool down more rapidly. One final thought – time is of the essence, no matter what the weather conditions. Your deer belongs in a cooler where the aging process can start, not in the bed of a truck or on a carrier where it is on prominent display. If you've got a bragging buck, there will be time enough for any buddies to admire it while it is hanging.

The Aging Process

Once you have completed the field-dressing process, it is time to start aging your deer. There are a number of options when it comes to just how this is done. Ideally, you want to hang the deer, with the hide still intact, for a minimum of five days in temperatures in the 38 to 40 degrees Fahrenheit range. Many commercial processors want no part of leaving the hide on or of "in-cooler" times beyond two or three days. This is understandable, since theirs is a seasonal operation where time (and space) means money.

Should you have the luxury to do your own aging, though, give it plenty of time and keep the hide on the animal. Time means tenderness when it comes to aging, and having the hide in place means that the flesh won't dry out and that, when it comes time, working the meat up will be a bit easier when it comes to removing silver skin. In cold-weather climates, it is often possible to hang a deer in a garage or storage room where you can keep the temperature low. However, temperatures below freezing do not help, for a frozen carcass has no opportunity to age or tenderize.

Yet another approach to aging, and it comes into play for money-conscious hunters in southern latitudes who want to do their own processing yet have no access to a cooler, is to age the meat after cutting up the deer. To do this, just skin the deer the way any processor will do it, using a gambrel and plenty of elbow grease or the golf ball method whereby you pull the hide away with help from a vehicle. Whatever your approach, take care to keep hair away from the carcass. Once you have the animal skinned, wash any vestiges of blood away and cut away any damaged or colored meat where the bullet entered and exited the deer. Then, depending on its size, you can age the meat in a cooler. If necessary, bone it out first. Just place the meat above any ice, keeping it from contact with a rack, platform or in some other fashion. You do not want the meat in direct contact with the ice. Check once a day or so, turning the meat if necessary to keep it evenly cooled. In a good cooler, the air temperature will be just about what you want, and one advantage of this system is that it lets you age the meat for whatever period you deem suitable.

In general terms, the longer you can age a whitetail's carcass, up to 10 days or so, the more tender the meat will become. For yearlings, and younger deer in general, the aging process doesn't need to be as lengthy. When it comes to aging, don't expect miracles. Old mossy horns will never become as tender as a Holstein that has been grain fed and finds it a struggle to walk across a quarter mile of pasture, but meat that is properly aged and suitably processed need not be so tough that your jaw muscles get an unwelcome workout every time you eat it.

Proper Processing

When it comes to processing, you have a world of choices. They begin with a decision as to whether you will handle the processing yourself or have it done commercially. Sometimes it is possible to purchase cooler time and handle the processing in person, but in our experience at least, most processors prefer to handle both the aging and processing as part of the whole package. Many will also gut the animal, but unless you can get the deer from the field to the abattoir in a period under an hour, field dressing is the way to go.

For those who process the deer in person, there are both advantages and disadvantages. On the plus side of matters, you know that the meat is actually that from the deer you shot. All too often, unethical processors just give you a "guesstimate" of the proper amount of meat, and you don't know what deer it came from. Furthermore, when you work the meat up in person, you will be able to take every care when it comes to removing silver skin, fat, damaged flesh and the like (such as the little glands found between the major muscle groups in the hind quarters). That translates to clean meat, no hair and complete confidence in the sanitary procedures followed in processing. Of course, if you pay a competent, conscientious processor, you will get comparable treatment.

On the negative side of matters, it takes an appreciable investment to get all of the equipment needed to turn a deer into the type of cuts and preparations many of us like. At a minimum, you will need a good bone saw, suitable knives, a place to work up the meat, freezer bags and butcher's wrapping paper. If you want much more than roasts, steaks and stew meat, you also need a means of preparing cubed steaks, burger, sausage and the like. It also helps, particularly when it comes to freezer shelf life, to have the capacity to vacuum seal the meat (we have a Tilia Professional II FoodSaver unit that does this quite nicely, although the storage bags are a bit pricey).

When it comes to diversity of cuts and specialty items such as various kinds of sausage, the commercial processor offers much more than what the home processor can possibly do. They likely have the ability to quick freeze the meat, which is quite important since it appreciably reduces the amount of ice crystallization. Processors will also have all the equipment needed to do the job properly. That is why, at least for folks who live where whitetails abound and for

whom venison constitutes a major item in the family diet, a commercial processor may be the way to go. Some suggestions in that regard might be helpful.

Mainly, you need to ask questions and check things out in person. In the case of processed meats, such as summer sausage or jerky, ask to have a tasting sample. By all means, ask to see the interior of the room where the processing is done. If that area is "off limits," the processor probably should be too. If the area is too dirty for you to see, eating meat processed there is obviously an "iffy" proposition. Make absolutely sure that everything connected with prices is clear at the outset. Finding out, after the fact, that skinning costs more or that you pay an unexpected premium for specialty cuts or packaging can be a real irritant. Find out the precise nature of the packaging. Anything short of careful wrapping with freezer paper that is clearly labeled is unacceptable, and vacuum packaging is distinctly preferable. Ask for a list of processing options. At the very least, the processor should offer burger, roasts, steaks and cubed steak. Options for sausage and specialty meats (summer sausage, smoked meat, kielbasa, bratwurst, bologna, cheese sausage, jerky and the like) are a real plus. Don't forget to ask about how long the deer is aged and whether it is possible to have the aging done with the hide intact. To our way of thinking, it is worth paying a bit of a premium to have a few extra days of aging with the hide in place.

Storage

Unless you intend to host a big neighborhood gathering or to feed the multitudes, it will be necessary to put much of your venison in a freezer. That may seem a simple enough matter, but as anyone who owns a freezer knows, things have a way of getting pushed to the back or overlooked. You can avoid this by keeping a list of what you store and when you do it, checking it off as individual packages are used. Alternatively, make a point of clearing the freezer once a year. The time to do this is late summer or early fall. Hold a neighborhood barbeque, fix a feast for the members of your hunt club, give the remaining meat to a local soup kitchen or take some similar step. If you make a practice of clearing the freezer just prior to the opening of each season, you should be able to keep things in good order.

Final Thoughts

How a deer is handled from the time it is shot until the moment the cooking process starts can make all the difference when it comes to taste. When defrosting venison for cooking, do it the proper way. That doesn't mean grabbing a package from the freezer, throwing it in the microwave to thaw it, and proceeding with cooking. Instead of this sort of mishandling, plan a day or two in advance. Take the venison to be used from the freezer and place it in the refrigerator. One helpful tip in this regard is to place the frozen meat in a colander or other container that will allow the melting ice crystals and other fluids to drain away.

With venison that has been properly handled and processed from the field to the stove, oven or grill, you have meat that will produce healthy, hearty and tasty meals. Obviously, that should become your primary goal once the adrenalin high of a successful hunt has washed over you and the serious business of dealing with your deer lies before you. Do it right, and you will savor the fruits of the hunt for many months and many meals.

Chapter 2

Health-Smart Venison Cookery

According to what you read or the authority being consulted, we live in a keenly health-conscious country or in a nation populated by three generations of couch potatoes. Obviously, the truth lies somewhere between. There is no denying, however, that Americans have an interest in what they eat and how it affects them that at times seems to approach fixation. Certainly for those who pay attention to their diet, and all of us should, venison rates raves as a miracle meat.

The health-related virtues of venison are virtually limitless. For starters, you are eating meat from an animal that has never known any infusion of inoculants, steroids, dietary supplements, growth hormones or indeed anything artificial. Rather, its browse consists of what nature has to offer in the habitat where the whitetail happens to live. This varies with the season – succulent new growth in the greening-up days of spring; a wide variety of diet items in the abundance of summer's warm, sultry days; autumn's bounty in the form of mast such as acorns and beechnuts along with soft mast such as wild grapes, persimmons, "stolen" fruits including apples and pears from orchards and other foodstuffs that prepare deer for the rigors of the rut and coming winter; and whatever browse the lean, mean days of cold and snow happen to offer. The result of such a diet – and rest assured deer know what is most nutritious and will utilize the available foods that serve them best – is a healthy animal untainted by anything artificial. You will be eating meat that is jam-packed with protein and carrying only the minerals and vitamins provided by a natural diet.

Another key health-related attribute of deer focuses on the nature of the meat. Compared with domestic meats such as beef, venison contains little fat. Moreover, as we have seen, proper dressing and care of the meat involves removal of any fat that might be present. This consideration, along with the nature of how deer live, translates to a lean meat that is frequently the only "red" meat individuals with heart problems are supposed to consume. Venison is comparatively low in cholesterol, and when cooked with health in mind, deserves the "heart smart" designation one sees with increasing frequency on grocery store labels. Maybe a better way of stressing the health-eating benefits afforded by venison comes through some basic comparisons with beef. According to scientific studies, a 3.5-ounce serving of ground beef has 40 percent more calories, 125 percent more cholesterol and 225 percent more fat than the same amount of venison. Indeed, venison actually has less cholesterol than chicken and turkey.

In some senses, every recipe in this cookbook lends itself to health consciousness, thanks to the basic qualities of venison. However, as a couple easing along toward the so-called "golden years" at an appreciably faster pace than we might desire, we have become increasingly aware of the need to watch every aspect of our diet. Ongoing fights with cholesterol levels, waistlines that have somehow forgotten where they were three decades ago and gentle reminders from family physicians necessitate such awareness. As a good friend once commented: "Once you pass 50 years of age it's just patch, patch, patch." We may not be patching much, but the ravages of time cannot be denied. If you can fight Father Time and health issues by continuing to eat well, it makes good sense to do so.

That is precisely the philosophy underlying the recipes in this chapter. They vary appreciably, from soups and salads to steaks on the grill, but a common thread runs through every recipe. You will find low levels of sodium and the substitution of herbs and spices in place of salt. Incidentally, using too much salt with venison is almost as much of a sin as overcooking it. Salt in too large quantities tends to hide flavor rather than enhance it. You will also find sparse use of oil, and where it is used, just a brushing of olive oil tends to be the suggested way to go. That's one of the magical things about grilling, whether it involves a fine steak cut from the backstrap or burger. The heat of the grill seals in flavor and does a fine job of cooking without frying or heavy reliance on grease.

With many of the recipes you will find hints or tips that give you the option of making them even healthier. These may involve the use of salt substitutes, low-fat ingredients or other considerations. Admittedly, such substitutes sometimes affect taste in a negative fashion, but it is amazing what suitable spices can do when used intelligently. Incidentally, that's something to keep in mind not just in this chapter but also throughout the book. For example, if you are on a stringently enforced low-sodium diet, try salt substitutes in recipes calling for salt. With a bit of experimentation and willingness to adjust, chances are you'll find dishes pleasing to the palate that also meet your health needs.

We readily recognize that moderation and a good measure of common sense are the keys to a sensible diet. However, it sure does help when things taste good, and here are a whole bunch of dishes (there's even a pizza recipe!) that offer fine flavor while adhering to sound health guidelines. It might even be noted that most of them lend themselves to diets placing emphasis on low-carbohydrate approaches. The only exceptions, in fact, are "Creamy Mushroom Venison Stroganoff," "Sausage Pizza," "Pepper Steak" and "Teriyaki Venison." This quartet of recipes makes use of either pasta or rice.

Forget the answer to a catchy Wendy's ad of the late 1980s, "Where's the beef?" For the health smart, it lies not in a fat-laced, cholesterol-laden burger but in the sensible, scrumptious fare provided by venison. Now, on to the recipes …

Fajita Salad with Caramelized Onions

1 pound venison loin steak,
trimmed

Marinade and Dressing:

1/4 cup ketchup
1/4 cup fresh lime juice
1/4 teaspoon lime zest
2 tablespoons honey
2 tablespoons green onion,
chopped finely
2 tablespoons olive oil
2 tablespoons water
1/4 teaspoon red pepper flakes
1/4 teaspoon ground cumin
1/2 teaspoon kosher salt
(or to taste)

Onions:

1 medium sweet onion, thinly
sliced
1 tablespoon olive oil
1 pinch sugar

Salad:

1 bag (10 ounces) mixed
romaine/leaf lettuce greens
1 cup grape tomatoes, halved
1 avocado, chopped
1 cup cucumber, sliced
1/2 cup fresh mushrooms,
sliced
1 cup Cheddar cheese, grated
1 small can (2 1/4 ounces)
sliced black olives
1-1/2 cups corn chips, coarsely
crumbled

1 can (14 ounces) pinto beans,
drained and rinsed
1/4 cup green onions, sliced
1/4 cup sour cream

Combine ingredients for dressing/marinade in a measuring cup and mix well.

Place steak in a glass dish and pour 1/4 cup dressing over steak. Turn steak to cover well. Marinate for 15-30 minutes or up to 2 hours. Refrigerate if marinating longer than 30 minutes, otherwise it may be marinated at room temperature.

Place 1 tablespoon olive oil in non-stick frying pan and heat to medium-high. Add onions and a pinch of sugar. Stir onions quickly, reduce heat and cook until dark golden brown. Allow 15-20 minutes for onions to caramelize. Remove from pan and drain on a paper towel while cooling.

Prepare ingredients for the salad, but keep components separate.

Remove steak from marinade and pat gently with a paper towel to remove part of the marinade. Discard the excess marinade. Season steak with salt and black pepper to taste. Sear steak on both sides until medium rare, 3-4 minutes per side. You can cook the steak on a grill, in a grilling pan, or even a non-stick skillet over high heat; however, take care that it does not scorch. Transfer meat to a cutting board and let rest for 5 minutes. Then, thinly slice steak against the grain with a sharp knife.

Fajita Salad with Caramelized Onions *(cont.)*

To assemble, layer half the salad greens in a deep glass bowl (a 12-inch trifle bowl is perfect). On the lettuce, layer half of each of the other salad ingredients (you can customize the ingredients to fit your needs), steak and caramelized onion slices. Drizzle with half the dressing, and then layer the rest of the ingredients. Pile the other half of the steak slices and onions in the center and drizzle remaining dressing on top. Top with sour cream and serve. This spectacular presentation makes the ordinary special.

Serves 4

Grilled Peppered Steaks

1/2 teaspoon garlic powder

1 teaspoon onion salt

1/2 teaspoon dried thyme

1 teaspoon ground black pepper

1 teaspoon Montreal Steak Seasoning

1/2 teaspoon Hungarian paprika

1/4 teaspoon crushed red pepper

1 teaspoon dried parsley flakes

4 venison loin steaks

8 teaspoons olive oil

Mix all dry ingredients together. Pour 1 teaspoon olive oil on each side of each steak and spread oil well. Pat seasonings onto steaks. Adjust the amount of seasonings used to increase or decrease the desired heat. Let steaks set for 30 minutes. Drizzle a little more olive oil on each steak.

Place steaks on a hot grill and cook quickly, about 3 minutes per side until medium rare. Do not overcook. Remove steaks from grill, lightly cover with foil and allow steaks to rest for 5 minutes before cutting. The resting time enables the juices to become evenly distributed throughout the steaks.

Serves 4

Burgers with Balsamic Caramelized Onions

Onions:

1 tablespoon olive oil
1 large onion, sliced
1 teaspoon sugar
1/4-1/2 teaspoon balsamic
vinegar
1/4 teaspoon kosher salt

Burgers:

1 pound ground venison
1 tablespoon dried parsley (or
1/4 cup fresh chopped
parsley)
2 tablespoon tomato paste
1 teaspoon Montreal Steak
Seasoning
1/2 teaspoon kosher salt
1/4 teaspoon freshly ground
black pepper
1-1/2 teaspoons olive oil

Cook onion and sugar in hot oil in a large non-stick skillet over low heat, stirring often, for 20 to 25 minutes or until onion is caramel colored. Stir in vinegar and salt. Set mixture aside and keep warm.

Combine ground venison, parsley, tomato paste and seasonings; gently shape into 4 patties. Brush with olive oil. Grill, covered with grill lid, over medium-high heat (350-400 degrees) 5 minutes per side or until desired doneness is reached. Serve open face on grilled garlic Texas toast with basil mayonnaise, caramelized onions and tomato slices.

Serves 4

Tips: You can give low-fat or non-fat mayonnaise a flavor boost by stirring in 1/2 cup with any of these ingredients:

Basil
1/2 cup fresh basil leaves, chopped

Dried Tomato
6 dried tomatoes, packed in oil, drained and minced

Lemon
1 teaspoon grated lemon rind
2 tablespoons fresh lemon juice

Caper
2 tablespoons chopped fresh parsley
2 tablespoons green onions, minced
1 tablespoon chopped capers
1 teaspoon hot sauce

Roasted Red Pepper
1/4 cup chopped roasted sweet red pepper

Onion
1/2 cup chopped onion, sautéed in 1 teaspoon olive oil

Creamy Mushroom Venison Stroganoff

1 package (8 ounces) egg
   noodles or pasta
1-1/2 pounds venison cubed
   steak, cut into thin strips
3 tablespoons olive oil
1/2 large sweet onion, chopped
1 garlic clove, minced
1 package (8 ounces) fresh
   mushrooms, sliced
2 tablespoons all-purpose flour
1 bouillon cube
1-1/2 cups water
3 teaspoons tomato paste
1/2 teaspoon paprika
1/2 teaspoon Worcestershire
   sauce
1 teaspoon kosher salt
1/2 teaspoon freshly ground
   black pepper
1/4 teaspoon dried basil
2 tablespoons dried parsley
3 heaping tablespoons
   reduced-fat sour cream

Cook noodles or pasta according to package directions.

Heat olive oil in a large non-stick skillet over medium-high heat and cook venison strips just until browned. You may need to cook the venison in batches. Do not crowd in the pan. Remove venison strips from pan and set aside.

Add onion to skillet and sauté about 2 minutes. Add garlic and sauté 30 seconds. Add mushrooms and sauté 3 minutes. Sprinkle with flour and stir until blended. Dissolve bouillon in hot water and add to mushrooms. Add tomato paste and cook, stirring constantly, until thickened.

Return venison to skillet and add paprika, Worcestershire sauce, salt, pepper, basil and parsley. Reduce heat and simmer about 15 minutes or until venison is tender. Remove from heat and stir in sour cream. Garnish with parsley. Serve over noodles or pasta.

Serves 4

Tip: Tossed salad, bread sticks and zinfandel wine complete the meal very nicely.

Italian Vegetable Soup

1 tablespoon olive oil
1 cup onion, chopped
1 garlic clove, minced
1/2 pound ground venison
1/2 cup carrots, sliced
1/2 cup celery, chopped
1 small zucchini, sliced
1 can (14 ounces) diced
  tomatoes
1 can (8 ounces) tomato sauce
1 can (16 ounces) red kidney
  beans, undrained
1 can (14 ounces) beef broth
1/2 - 3/4 cup water
1 tablespoon dried parsley
  flakes
1/2 teaspoon kosher salt
1/2 teaspoon oregano
1/2 teaspoon sweet basil
1/4 teaspoon thyme
1/4 teaspoon marjoram
1/4 teaspoon black pepper,
  freshly ground
2 cups chopped cabbage
1 can (8 ounces) green beans,
  drained
1/2 cup small elbow macaroni
Parmesan or Romano cheese as
  garnish

Pour olive oil in large, heavy kettle and heat to medium high. Add onions and sauté until tender (3 - 4 minutes). Add garlic and sauté 1 minute. Add ground venison and cook until venison is no longer pink. Add all other ingredients except cabbage, green beans and macaroni. Bring to a boil. Lower heat; cover and simmer 15 minutes. Add cabbage, green beans and macaroni. Return to simmer and cook until vegetables and pasta are tender (about 10 minutes). Sprinkle with Parmesan cheese before serving.

Serves 10-12

Tips: If you prefer a meatier soup, additional ground venison can be used. This is a healthy soup. To make the soup more heart healthy use low-sodium, no-salt-added, reduced-fat canned items. Whole-wheat pasta is a healthier choice.

Summertime Okra Soup

1 tablespoon olive oil
1/2 pound ground venison
1 medium onion, chopped
2 cups low sodium chicken
   broth
2 cups fresh chopped okra
4 cups peeled and chopped
   fresh tomatoes
1/2 teaspoon kosher salt
1/4 teaspoon black pepper
1/2 teaspoon sugar
2 cups fresh corn
1 teaspoon beef base
1 cup cooked crowder peas,
   optional

Heat olive oil in a Dutch oven and brown venison and onion. Add chicken broth, okra, tomatoes, salt, pepper and sugar. Simmer for 15 minutes. Add corn, beef base and crowder peas (if using). Simmer for 10 additional minutes. Taste and adjust seasonings.

Serves 10-12

Tips: Beef base enhances the flavor and can be found with Tone's spices at stores such as Sam's or Costco. Tomatoes and okra is a traditional Southern dish. Combining them with venison adds another dimension.

Northern Bean Soup

2 tablespoons olive oil
1/2 cup chopped onion
1 cup chopped carrots
2 garlic cloves, minced
1/2 pound venison kielbasa,
   cut into chunks
3 cups chicken broth
1/2 teaspoon dried Italian
   seasoning
1/2 teaspoon freshly ground
   black pepper
1 can (16 ounces) Great
   Northern Beans, drained and
   rinsed
4 ounces fresh baby spinach
   (or 1/4 package frozen
   spinach)
Grated Romano cheese

Heat olive oil in a large sauce pan over medium-high heat. Add onion, carrots, garlic and kielbasa; sauté about 5 minutes. Add broth, Italian seasoning, pepper and beans. Bring to a boil, reduce heat and simmer until carrots are tender (about 5 minutes). Add spinach, stirring until spinach wilts. Top with grated Romano cheese.

Serves 4

Sausage Pizza

1 can (8 ounces) reduced-fat
refrigerated crescent dinner
roll dough
1 tablespoon olive oil
3/4 pound bulk venison
sausage
1-1/2 cups frozen shredded
hash brown potatoes,
thawed
1/4 cup fat free milk
1/2 cup broccoli, cooked
1-1/2 to 2 cups shredded
Cheddar cheese (fat free can
be used)
1/2 teaspoon kosher salt
1/4 teaspoon black pepper
1 carton (8 ounces) egg
substitute
2 tablespoons grated fresh
Parmesan cheese

Preheat oven to 375 degrees.
Separate dough into triangles and
press triangles together to form a
single round crust on a 12-inch
pizza pan coated evenly with olive
oil.
Crimp edges of dough with
fingers to form a rim.
Cook sausage in a large, non-
stick skillet over medium heat until
browned. Stir to crumble.
Top prepared dough with
sausage, potatoes, broccoli and
cheese. Combine milk, salt, pepper
and egg substitute, stirring with a
whisk. Carefully pour milk/egg
mixture over sausage mixture.
Sprinkle with Parmesan cheese.
Bake at 375 degrees for 25-30
minutes or until crust is browned.

Serves 4 - 6

*Tips: Fresh broccoli can be cooked quickly in the microwave. Frozen
broccoli does not need to be pre-cooked but does need to be thawed
before adding to the pizza. Take time to make a good rim on the crust
to prevent the milk/egg mixture from running. This pizza makes a
nice brunch or breakfast and is delicious as a light supper with a
salad. Venison sausage is a much leaner choice than pork.*

Eric's Special Steak

3 - 4 venison steaks

Marinade:

1/4 cup Dale's Steak Seasoning

1/2 cup water

1 tablespoon Worcestershire sauce

1 tablespoon A-1 Steak Sauce

1/2 tablespoon another steak sauce such as Heinz 57, London Steak Sauce or Crosse and Blackwell Steak Sauce

Mix marinade ingredients well and marinate venison steaks 3 - 4 hours. Grill to desired doneness, allow steaks to rest for 5 minutes and serve. Do not overcook steaks; they should still be pink on the inside.

Serves 3 - 4

Tip: The secret is to use different kinds of steak sauces for a blend of flavors.

Dijon Loin Steaks

Batter:

1/3 cup Dijon mustard
3 tablespoons water
2 teaspoons Worcestershire
  sauce
1 garlic clove, minced
1/2 teaspoon Italian seasoning

1 pound venison loin steaks
1 cup dry, fine bread crumbs
  (from whole wheat bread)
2 tablespoons canola oil

Combine all batter ingredients and mix well; place in a shallow dish. Place bread crumbs in a second shallow dish. Dip venison loin steaks first in batter to coat and then dredge in bread crumbs.

Place 2 tablespoons canola oil in a non-stick skillet and cook steaks over medium-high heat. Cook about 5 minutes or until golden brown on both sides. Do not overcook and turn only once. Steaks should still be pink in the center.

Serves 4

Worcestershire Steaks

3 - 4 venison steaks

Marinade:

1/4 cup Worcestershire sauce
1/4 cup olive oil
2 tablespoons lemon juice
1/2 teaspoon onion salt
1 garlic clove, minced
1/2 teaspoon black pepper

Mix marinade ingredients and place in a resealable plastic bag. Add steaks and marinate 3 - 4 hours in the refrigerator. Grill steaks over hot coals or broil until desired degree of doneness is reached. Do not overcook. About 4 - 5 minutes per side is usually adequate.

Serves 3 - 4

Pepper Steak

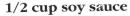

1/2 cup soy sauce
1 teaspoon sugar
1 garlic clove, minced
1 pound venison steak, cut into strips
2 tablespoons olive oil
1 large green pepper, cut into strips
1 red onion, thinly sliced
1 cup sliced fresh mushrooms
1/2 cup water
2 tablespoons cornstarch

Combine soy sauce, sugar and garlic. Add venison steak, which has been cut into strips. Toss lightly and refrigerate 3 - 4 hours. Drain steak.

In a heavy skillet or wok, add oil and heat to medium high; add venison strips and stir fry 3 - 4 minutes; add pepper, onion and mushrooms and stir fry for 3 - 4 additional minutes or until vegetables are tender crisp. Combine water and cornstarch and add to meat and vegetables, stirring constantly until thickened. Serve over rice, pasta or mashed potatoes.

Teriyaki Venison

1 pound cubed venison steaks, cut into thin strips

Marinade:

1/2 cup soy sauce
2 tablespoons brown sugar
1 garlic clove, minced
1/4 teaspoon ground ginger

Steak and Vegetables:

2 tablespoons olive oil
2 tablespoons butter
1 small onion, sliced
1 cup fresh mushrooms, sliced
1 cup bell pepper strips

Mix soy sauce, brown sugar, garlic and ginger; add steak strips. Marinate for 30 - 45 minutes. Heat oil and butter and sauté vegetables until tender. Push to side of pan and add venison steak strips, which have been drained well. Sauté until steak is done and serve over rice.

Serves 4

Grilled Loin Steaks

1 venison loin, cut into
   1-inch-thick steaks

Marinade:

1 cup low-sodium soy sauce
1 large garlic clove, minced
1 tablespoon honey
1 tablespoon steak sauce
   (your choice)
Several dashes Tabasco sauce

Cut loin into steaks. Place steaks in a resealable plastic bag. Mix marinade ingredients well and pour into the bag over steaks. Marinate in the refrigerator for 3 - 4 hours. Place on a grill or use grilling pan and cook on medium-high heat to desired doneness. Do not overcook.

Tips: Do not have the heat too high or the marinade will burn on the exterior of the steaks. The touch of honey adds a great deal to the flavor but does tend to burn if the heat is high.

Chili Steak and Salsa

1 teaspoon chili powder
1 - 2 garlic cloves, finely
    minced
1/2 teaspoon kosher salt
1/2 teaspoon black pepper
3/4 - 1 pound cubed venison
    steaks
1 tablespoon olive oil
1/4 – 1/2 cup salsa

Combine chili powder, garlic, salt and pepper. Rub evenly into both sides of steaks. Place 1 tablespoon oil in a non-stick skillet over medium heat until hot. Add steaks and cook to desired degree of doneness (about 8 minutes). Turn steaks to brown evenly. Serve with salsa placed on top of each steak.

Salsa:

2 large tomatoes, chopped
2 tablespoons minced fresh
    Cilantro
1/2 cup thinly sliced green
    onions
1 fresh jalapeno pepper, seeded
    and finely chopped
1 garlic clove, minced
2 tablespoon olive oil
3 tablespoons fresh lime juice
1/2 teaspoon salt
1/8 teaspoon black pepper

Combine all ingredients in a large bowl; mix well. Cover and refrigerate for several hours to blend flavors.

Hamburger Steak with Onion Topping

2 tablespoons canola oil
1 – 1-1/2 cups sliced sweet
   onions
1 - 2 tablespoons water
1/4 teaspoon paprika
Black pepper to taste
1 pound ground venison
Salt to taste

Heat canola oil in a large skillet and sauté onions until tender. Add water while sautéing onions if needed to prevent sticking. Stir paprika and black pepper into onions; remove onions from pan and keep warm. Season ground venison with salt and shape into 2 large 1-inch-thick patties. Put hamburger steaks in onion-flavored oil and cook over medium heat until browned on both sides and desired doneness is reached. Arrange steaks on 2 plates and top with reserved, cooked onions.

Serves 2

Chapter 3
Fancy Fixings

Mention venison to the vast majority of the population who has no experience either as hunters or in dining on wild game, and you typically get one of two reactions. Most dismiss venison offhand, suggesting the meat is tough, "gamey," dry and generally unpalatable. Others associate the meat with backwoods hunt camps, stews or pots of chili of dubious culinary distinction, or hunters whose idea of gourmet fare is a double cheeseburger. Such thinking is as prevalent as it is singularly wrongheaded. Sadly, it prevails to a surprising degree even among hardcore deer hunters.

Simply put, whether judged from the perspective of taste or nutrition, venison can provide dishes fit for a king. Indeed, in European countries throughout the Middle Ages and beyond, such was precisely the case. Deer hunting was a privilege reserved for royalty, and poaching could be punished by death. Even today, the sport remains the exclusive preserve of the affluent and well-connected over most of the world. One of the distinguishing characteristics of being an American is the right not only to bear arms but to also use them to hunt. Today, more than any other type of hunting, the whitetail quest is America's sport. The animal is more plentiful than ever, and all across the country, hunters have ample opportunity to put venison in the freezer and on the table.

If simple soups, stews, burgers and chili suit all your expectations when it comes to eating, certainly that's fine. Yet, what was once the food of kings can still be prepared in ways fit for a king or the most discriminating of palates. It is no accident that farm-raised venison has increasingly become available, and it regularly appears on the menu in high-dollar restaurants. In foreign countries, most notably New Zealand, venison production has become big business thanks to greatly expanded demand in elite culinary circles.

We don't fit in such circles, either economically or from the standpoint of being elitist in our tastes, but that doesn't mean that we don't enjoy sitting down to truly fancy fixings. In the part of the world where we live, the South, venison has long been associated with feasts and special occasions. For example, one of the finest and most prolific outdoor writers this country has produced, South Carolina's Archibald Rutledge, thought no Christmas family gathering at his beloved Hampton Plantation was complete without venison. Or look at what a friend once described as "Christmas in September," the opening day of dove season. A feast that resembles nothing so much as a cross between a family reunion and an all-day singing with dinner on the grounds forms an integral part of most serious Southern dove shoots. You can count on the aroma of haunches of venison sitting atop a big barbeque outfit or

loin steaks sizzling on the grill being as much a part of such occasions as the smell of burnt powder drifting across the sere fields of September.

Participants in such occasions recognize that venison is not only delicious but also eminently worthy of a place of honor on even the most festive of tables. The recipes that follow pay tribute to the finer qualities (and cuts) of venison. They offer recognition of the fact that the meat lends itself to creativity and to preparation of really special dishes. Much of our emphasis involves ingredients that mix and marry wonderfully well with venison – various types of seafood, certain spices, fruits and berries, wine and the like. The preparation time for some of these recipes may seem a bit long or the level of cooking skill involved fairly high. Rest assured, though, that the end results are well worthwhile, and you will find adventures into the world of fine dining a delightful experience. In that regard, I would re-emphasize the fact that the two of us, as authors and as people, are simple folks at heart. Neither of us has any formal culinary training, and while we certainly enjoy dining in a fine restaurant on rare occasions, neither of us qualifies as a discerning gourmet by any stretch of the imagination. Yet for us, and we believe for countless other deer hunters and fellow lovers of nature's incredible bounty as well, sitting down to a meal that my grandfather would have described as "sho nuff fancy fixin's" brings a meaningful measure of dining pleasure. We hope that the recipes that follow enable you to share similar pleasures.

Venison Loin Steaks with Shrimp Gravy over Garlic Cheese Grits

Steaks:

1 pound venison loin steaks
2 tablespoons olive oil
1 teaspoon Lawry's Lemon and
   Lime Pepper

Gravy:

1 pound peeled and deveined
   shrimp
1 medium onion, chopped
4 strips bacon
1-1/2 teaspoon Worcestershire
   sauce
1/4 teaspoon kosher salt
1/8 teaspoon freshly ground
   black pepper
2 tablespoons flour
1 cup water

Grits:

1 cup chicken broth
1/2 cup half and half
1/2 cup water
1/4 cup butter
1 clove garlic, minced
1/2 teaspoon kosher salt
1/4 teaspoon freshly ground
   black pepper
1 cup quick cooking grits
3/4 cup shredded Cheddar
   cheese

Drizzle olive oil over steaks and sprinkle with Lemon and Lime seasoning. Let steaks marinate for 1 hour.

Cook bacon in skillet until crisp and remove from pan. Quickly brown steaks in bacon drippings and remove from pan, cover with foil and let steaks rest while making the shrimp gravy.

Sauté onions in bacon drippings. Add shrimp (well drained), Worcestershire sauce, salt and pepper, stirring constantly. When shrimp start to turn pink, sprinkle in flour until shrimp are well coated. Add water, stirring constantly until gravy is the consistency you desire. Crumble bacon and add. Simmer no longer than 4 minutes after adding flour. Correct seasonings if necessary.

For grits, bring first 7 ingredients to a boil in a large sauce pan over medium heat. Stir in grits; cover, reduce heat and cook, stirring often, for 5 - 6 minutes. Remove from heat, add cheese and stir to melt cheese.

Place a mound of grits on a plate, top with steak and spoon shrimp gravy over all. Serve immediately.

Serves 4 - 6

Venison Loin Steaks with Shrimp Gravy over Garlic Cheese Grits *(cont.)*

Tips: Grilled grits are a delicious way to use the leftovers. Place grits in a lightly greased pan and refrigerate overnight. Grits will become stiff. Cut grits into squares, brush both sides well with olive oil and grill for 4 - 5 minutes per side or until golden brown. Be sure you oil the grill rack well also. The grits are crunchy on the exterior and creamy inside. These can also be cooked in a skillet if desired. Try these grits with barbecue, fried fish, or dry rubs.

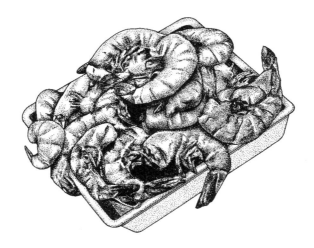

Loin Steaks with Mango Salsa

1 pound venison loin steaks,
cut into 1/2-inch thick steaks

2 tablespoons olive oil

Salt and pepper to taste

Drizzle olive oil over steaks and season with salt and pepper. Let steaks marinate for 30 minutes while grill heats. Grill steaks quickly; do not overcook. Steaks should be pink inside. Serve steaks topped with mango salsa.

Salsa:

1/2 lemon
1 large ripe mango, peeled and
cut into 1/2-inch chunks
3 tablespoons sweet onion,
finely minced
1/2 cup seedless cucumber,
chopped
1 tablespoon fresh mint leaves,
chopped
4 blades fresh chives, finely
chopped
1/8 teaspoon salt

Grate 1/2 teaspoon peel from lemon and squeeze 1 tablespoon juice. In medium bowl, toss lemon peel and juice with mango, cucumber, mint, chives and salt. Cover and refrigerate up to 2 hours if not serving immediately.

Tip: Soak onion in iced water for 10 minutes to remove some of the sharpness.

Loin Steaks with Bourbon Marinade and Dipping Sauce

Marinade and Sauce:

1-1/4 cups chili sauce
  (1 12-ounce bottle)
1/4 cup finely chopped chives
1/4 cup olive oil
2 tablespoons maple syrup
2 tablespoons bourbon
2 tablespoons Worcestershire
  sauce
2 tablespoons low-sodium soy
  sauce
1 teaspoon horseradish
1 garlic clove, finely minced

Steaks:

1 pound venison loin steaks,
  cut 3/4-inch thick

For marinade, whisk all ingredients together in a small bowl.

Place steaks in a resealable plastic bag and pour 1 cup of marinade over them. Reserve the remainder of the marinade and refrigerate. Marinate steaks in the refrigerator for 3 - 4 hours.

Grill or broil steaks until desired doneness is reached. Do not overcook; steaks should be pink inside. Serve steaks with reserved sauce for dipping.

Serves 4

Tips: Bottled chili sauce resembles ketchup and can be found in the condiment section of your supermarket. This marinade is a delightfully different flavor combination that offers the best of two worlds inasmuch as it can be used as a marinade or dip. The versatile sauce nicely compliments venison steaks. It can also be used on doves, duck, shrimp, pork, chicken or beef.

Southwestern Venison Loin Steak Wraps

1 tablespoon chili powder
1 teaspoon cumin
1/2 teaspoon dry mustard
1/2 teaspoon garlic powder
1/2 teaspoon kosher salt
1/2 teaspoon black pepper
2 tablespoons olive oil

10-12 ounces venison loin
steak

4 tortillas, heated

In a small bowl combine chili powder, cumin, dry mustard, garlic powder, salt and pepper. Mix well. Drizzle olive oil over steak and spread seasoning rub evenly over steak. Marinate steak in the refrigerator for 1 hour.

Place steak on a grill over medium heat and cook to desired doneness. Venison is best served medium rare and should not be overcooked. Let steak rest 10 minutes before slicing. Cut steak diagonally across grain into thin strips. Place steak strips on heated tortillas, top with salsa of your choice and roll to form a wrap. Peach salsa compliments the venison but a more traditional tomato salsa (see recipe below) can be used.

Tomato Salsa:

2 cups fresh tomatoes, seeded
and chopped
1 garlic clove, minced
1/4 cup sliced green onions
1 fresh jalapeño pepper, seeded
and finely chopped
2 tablespoons fresh-squeezed
lime juice
1/4 teaspoon kosher salt
1/8 teaspoon freshly ground
black pepper
2 tablespoons fresh chopped
cilantro

Combine all ingredients well and chill until ready to serve.

Greek Steak Pitas
with Cucumber Dill Sauce

Sauce:

1 container (8 ounces) plain
  yogurt
1 teaspoon dried dill weed
1/4 teaspoon Greek seasoning
2/3 cup finely chopped
  cucumber
1 garlic clove, minced
1/4 teaspoon kosher salt
1/4 teaspoon freshly ground
  black pepper

Marinade:

1/4 cup fresh lemon juice
2 tablespoons olive oil
1 teaspoon Greek seasoning
1 garlic clove, minced
1/4 teaspoon kosher salt
1/2 teaspoon freshly ground
  black pepper

1 pound venison steak,
  trimmed and cut into narrow
  strips
4 pitas (6-inch), cut in half
Romaine lettuce leaves
1/2 cup crumbled feta cheese

To prepare sauce, combine all ingredients and stir well.

To prepare steak marinade, combine juice, olive oil and next 4 ingredients. Mix ingredients well with a wire whisk and pour into a resealable plastic bag. Add venison steak, which has been cut into thin strips. Marinate 10-15 minutes.

Drain steak and place in a large frying pan and sauté for several minutes until steak strips are medium rare. If your pan is not crowded, it takes only 2-3 minutes for the steak strips to cook.

Line each pita half with a lettuce leaf and divide steak evenly among pita halves. Spoon cucumber dill sauce and feta cheese into each pita half and serve.

Serves 4

Tips: If you do not have Greek seasoning, dried oregano can be substituted. A marinated tomato salad compliments the pita steak sandwiches.

Three Country Surf and Turf

Steaks:

1 pound venison steak, cut into thin strips
2 tablespoons olive oil
Cavender's All-purpose Greek Seasoning

10-12 corn tortillas (6 inch)

Sauce:

2 tablespoons butter
2 tablespoons finely minced onion
3 tablespoons flour
2 cups milk
1/2 cup heavy cream
1/8 teaspoon allspice
1/2 teaspoon salt
1/8 teaspoon black pepper
1-1/2 cups Fontina or Swiss cheese, grated
1/2 - 1 cup Cheddar cheese, shredded
1 pound cooked and peeled shrimp

Cut steaks into thin strips, drizzle with olive oil and sprinkle with Greek seasoning. Marinate steaks for 30 minutes.

Meanwhile, prepare sauce. Melt butter in a sauce pan over medium heat and sauté onion until tender. Add flour and cook for 1 minute, stirring constantly. Gradually add milk and cream, stirring constantly until sauce is thickened. Add allspice, salt and pepper. Stir in Fontina cheese and shrimp.

Reserve one half of sauce, add cheddar cheese to reserved sauce and warm until cheese just melts.

Place steak strips in frying pan and quickly sauté until browned but still pink in the center.

Soften tortillas by wrapping in a damp paper towel and microwave for 30 - 40 seconds.

To assemble, place steak strips down center of tortillas, cover with several spoons of shrimp sauce, roll tortillas, and place in a greased casserole dish seam side down. When all tortillas have been rolled, pour reserved sauce (with Cheddar cheese) down middle of tortillas making a lengthwise band across tortillas.

Bake at 350 degrees for 20 - 25 minutes or until hot and bubbly.

Serves 6 - 8

Three Country Surf and Turf *(cont.)*

Tips: This is a very unusual combination of flavors, but the end result is most appealing. If desired, crepes can be used instead of tortillas. Other cooked seafood, such as crab, scallops or firm white fish can be added or used instead of the shrimp.

Ches's Chops

1 pound venison chops or
  steaks
1/2 cup teriyaki sauce
1/2 cup orange juice
1 teaspoon ground ginger

Place venison chops or steaks in a resealable plastic bag. Mix teriyaki sauce, orange juice and ginger thoroughly in a small bowl. Pour marinade mixture over chops and seal bag. Remove as much excess air as possible from bag while sealing. Place in refrigerator and marinate at least 24 hours; turn bag several times. Drain chops well and place on a hot grill cooking until chops are medium rare.

Venison with Lobster Cream Sauce

Venison:

8 venison steak cutlets,
   pounded thin
2 tablespoons butter
2 tablespoons olive oil
1/4 – 1/2 cup flour
Salt and pepper to taste
Juice of 1 lemon

Sauce:

2 tablespoons finely minced
   sweet onion
2 tablespoons butter
3 tablespoons flour
1/2 cup white wine
1/2 cup heavy cream
1-1/2 cups milk
1/8 teaspoon allspice
1/2 teaspoon black pepper
Salt to taste
1 package (8 ounces) imitation
   lobster meat

Melt butter in a sauce pan over medium heat. Sauté onion in butter until tender. Add flour to make a roux; gradually add wine, cream and milk, stirring constantly. Add allspice, salt and pepper. Simmer, stirring constantly until thick. Add imitation lobster.

Heat butter and oil in a frying pan. Season flour with salt and pepper. Dip cutlets in seasoned flour and cook 2 - 3 minutes; turn, sprinkle with lemon juice and cook until browned but still pink in the center. Transfer cutlets to plates, top with lobster sauce and serve.

Serves 8

Tip: Sometimes it is nice to splurge and use real lobster.

Venison Teriyaki

1 bottle (10 ounces) soy sauce
2-1/2 cups water (20 ounces-
rinse soy bottle twice)
1/4 teaspoon ground ginger
3/4 teaspoon sugar
3/4 teaspoon vinegar
1/2 teaspoon garlic powder,
or to taste

1 venison loin, sliced across
the grain and 1/4-inch thick

Combine first six ingredients well. Slice venison thinly and place in a large resealable storage bag or glass dish. Marinate in refrigerator for 24 hours; turn venison several times while marinating.

Preheat grill to medium high. Drain venison slices and place on oiled grill. Cook venison quickly until medium rare, being careful not to overcook. Thin slices will take only a few minutes.

Tips: It is much easier to slice the venison thinly if the loin is partially frozen. If you tailgate or picnic with a grill, this would be an excellent choice for a quick and tasty main dish.

Merlot Loin

1 large garlic clove, minced

1 teaspoon freshly ground black pepper

1/2 teaspoon Italian seasoning

2 teaspoons olive oil

1 venison loin, cut into 1-inch-thick steaks

2 tablespoons olive oil

2 tablespoons butter, divided (no substitution)

2 tablespoons chopped onion

1/2 cup sliced mushrooms

1/2 cup beef bouillon

1/4 cup merlot wine

1 teaspoon Worcestershire sauce

Place minced garlic, pepper, Italian seasoning and 2 teaspoons olive oil in a bowl and mix well. Rub into loin steaks and refrigerate for 2 - 3 hours.

Pour 2 tablespoons olive oil in a skillet and add 1 tablespoon butter. Heat to medium high and add steaks. Cook about 4 minutes per side. Do not overcook. Centers of steaks should be pink. Remove steaks from the pan and add onion and mushrooms. Sauté briefly and add beef bouillon, merlot wine and Worcestershire sauce. Increase heat to high and reduce liquid by half. Blend in 1 tablespoon butter and pour sauce over steaks.

Serves 3 - 4

 51

Loin Steaks with Raspberry Sauce

1 pound loin steaks, cut into
  1/2-inch thick steaks
1/3 cup Dale's steak seasoning
1/3 cup water
1/2 stick margarine or butter
1 garlic clove, minced
1/2 cup raspberry jam

Marinate loin in Dale's steak seasoning and water. Drain. Melt the margarine and add garlic. Sauté briefly. Add loin and cook to desired doneness. Remove loin and de-glaze pan with jam. Serve as sauce for dipping loin.

Venison Loin Medallions with Cherry Sauce

1 cup low-sodium chicken
  stock or broth
1 cup beef broth
1/2 cup cherry liqueur
1/3 cup red ruby cherry pie
  filling
1 tablespoon cornstarch
  dissolved in 1/4 cup water
3 tablespoons butter, divided
8 venison loin steak medallions
  (about 1/2-inch thick)

Combine chicken and beef stocks in small, heavy sauce pan. Boil until liquid is reduced to 1 cup (about 15 minutes). Add cherry liqueur and boil until liquid is reduced to 3/4 cup (about 5 minutes). Whisk in cherry-pie filling and simmer until sauce starts to thicken. Add 1 tablespoon cornstarch, which has been dissolved in 1/4 cup water, to sauce and stir until sauce thickens. Whisk in 1 tablespoon butter. Season sauce with salt and pepper if desired. Set aside.

Sprinkle venison with salt and pepper. Melt remaining 2 tablespoons butter in a large, non-stick skillet over medium-high heat. Add venison to skillet and cook to desired doneness. Place 2 medallions on each plate and top with cherry sauce.

Serves 4

Pineapple Garlic Loin Steak with Mushroom Sauce

**1 whole loin, cut into 1-inch-
thick steaks**

Pineapple Marinade:

**1 can (6 ounces) pineapple
juice
1 tablespoon teriyaki marinade
and sauce
1 garlic clove, minced**

Mushroom Sauce:

**3 tablespoons margarine or
butter
2 garlic cloves, minced
1-1/2 cups sliced fresh
mushrooms
1/4 teaspoon dried thyme
1/4 teaspoon dried parsley
1 cup chicken broth
1 teaspoon cornstarch
Salt and pepper to taste**

Mix marinade ingredients well and place loin steaks in marinade and refrigerate for 2 - 3 hours. Drain and quickly cook steaks in a grilling pan. Alternatively you can broil them or cook them on a grill. Cook until slightly pink in the center. Place cooked loin on a deep platter and cover with mushroom sauce.

For mushroom sauce, melt margarine and cook garlic about 20 seconds; add mushrooms and sauté until tender. Add herbs. Mix cornstarch and broth and add to mushrooms. Cook until thickened and smooth. Pour over steaks and serve immediately with garlic spaghetti.

Loin Steaks with Crab, Shrimp and Scallop Sauce

1 tablespoon olive oil
1 tablespoon butter
1 pound loin steaks, cut
    1/2-inch thick
Salt and pepper to taste

Sauce:

2 tablespoons olive oil
1/2 pound fresh mushrooms,
    sliced
2 cups whipping cream
1/4 cup White Zinfandel wine
1/4 cup butter, cut into 12
    pieces
1/2 pound crab meat
8 - 12 medium shrimp, cooked
    and shelled
6 - 8 sea scallops, cooked and
    chopped

For steaks, place olive oil and butter in a large skillet and quickly cook venison loin until medium rare. Keep steaks warm on a platter covered with foil. It is best to cook loin after sauce has started thickening.

For sauce, heat 2 tablespoons olive oil in a large skillet. Add mushrooms and sauté 5 minutes. Add cream and wine and reduce until thickened (about 10 - 12 minutes). Season with salt and pepper. Stir in butter one piece at a time, incorporating each piece completely before adding next. Add crab meat, shrimp and scallops; heat through, about 1 minute. Pour over venison and serve.

Serves 4

Loin Steaks with Apricot Mustard Sauce

4 - 6 venison loin steaks
Salt
Black pepper
Butter

Sauce:

1/2 cup grainy brown mustard
1/3 cup apricot jam
1/4 cup brandy

Heat a non-stick skillet over medium-high heat; sprinkle the skillet lightly with salt and add steak. Cook until browned and turn steak (sprinkling the pan with salt again before placing back in the pan). Cook until steak reaches desired doneness (do not overcook) and sprinkle with freshly ground black pepper. Top each steak with a small pat of butter and allow to melt into the steaks before removing from the pan.

Meanwhile, heat mustard, jam and brandy in a small sauce pan over medium heat, stirring frequently, until the jam has melted and ingredients are well combined. Drizzle sauce over steaks and serve immediately.

Serves 4

Tip: Baked apricots make a wonderful accompaniment to these steaks. Try them with doves or quail also.

Baked Apricots

1 can (16 ounces) apricot halves, drained
15 Ritz crackers, crushed
2 tablespoons light brown sugar
2 tablespoons butter, melted

Place drained apricots in a casserole dish. Roll crackers into crumbs. Sprinkle crackers on top of apricots. Sprinkle brown sugar over crackers and pour melted butter over top. Bake at 350 degrees about 15 - 20 minutes or until hot, bubbly and golden brown.

Serves 2 - 3

Tip: If you wish to make a larger casserole, alternate layers of apricots, crumbs and brown sugar.

Loin Steaks with Onion Relish

1 pound venison loin steaks,
  cut 3/4-inch thick
1/4 - 1 teaspoon coarsely
  ground black pepper
2 tablespoons olive oil
1 tablespoon margarine or
  butter
1 tablespoon lemon juice
1 large Vidalia onion, thinly
  sliced and separated into
  rings
1/2 cup zinfandel wine
1/2 teaspoon dried basil,
  crushed
1/4 teaspoon salt

Rub both sides of steaks with the ground pepper. In a large, non-stick skillet heat oil and margarine over medium-high heat; add steaks and cook about 4 minutes on each side for medium doneness. Remove the steaks and reserve drippings. Keep steaks warm by covering with foil.

Cook onion in drippings over medium heat for 5 - 7 minutes or until tender crisp. Add wine, basil and salt. Cook until most of the liquid has evaporated. Arrange steaks on plates and spoon onion relish on top.

Serves 4

Tips: Leftovers make good sandwiches. Try them topped with mozzarella cheese. Broil to heat and melt cheese.

Loin Steaks with Bourbon Cream Sauce

1 pound venison loin steaks
1 tablespoon olive oil
1 teaspoon Lawry's Steak and
Chop Seasoning and Rub

1 tablespoon olive oil
1 tablespoon butter

Sauce:

2 tablespoons minced onion
1/4 cup bourbon
1/2 cup beef broth
1/4 cup heavy (whipping)
cream
1/4 teaspoon black pepper
Pinch of salt

Drizzle 1 tablespoon olive oil over steaks and sprinkle with 1 teaspoon seasoning covering both sides of steaks.

Heat 1 tablespoon each olive oil and butter in a skillet over medium-high heat. Quickly brown steaks being careful not to overcook. Steaks should be pink inside. Remove steaks and cover with foil to keep warm.

In the same skillet that the steaks were cooked in, cook the onion over medium heat until softened, about 2 minutes. Add the bourbon and broth, increase heat to high and cook, stirring and scraping the pan constantly, until the sauce is reduced to half, 2 - 3 minutes. Reduce heat to medium and stir in cream, pepper and salt to taste; do not let the mixture boil.

Spoon sauce over steaks and serve immediately.

Peachy Barbecue Venison

1 pound can peach halves or
   slices
1 cup chili sauce
1/2 cup vinegar
1/4 cup Worcestershire sauce
1 garlic clove, minced
2 teaspoon beef base (or
   bouillon cubes)
1/4 cup butter
1 – 1-1/2 pounds venison flank
   (or rump) steak

Drain peaches and reserve syrup. Set aside.

In a sauce pan combine syrup, chili sauce, vinegar, Worcestershire sauce, garlic, beef base and butter. Bring to a boil, reduce heat and simmer 10 - 15 minutes.

Score steak by making shallow diagonal cuts in a diamond pattern. Place steak and peaches in a large dish. Cover with barbecue sauce (reserve 1/4 – 1/2 cup to use for a dipping sauce) and marinate 8 - 10 hours or overnight in the refrigerator.

Transfer steak only to a greased pan and broil 3 - 5 minutes. Turn steak. Add peaches (cut side up if you use halves). Baste steak and peaches. Broil 3 - 5 minutes longer or until steak is medium rare. Let steak rest 5 minutes to re-distribute juices. Arrange diagonally sliced steak and peaches on a platter. Serve with warm marinade sauce for dipping.

Serves 3

Tips: A grill can be used for this steak. Chili sauce is usually found near the ketchup at the supermarket and beef base is near the herbs and spices.

Venison Tenderloin with Tomato Basil Sauce

4 venison loin steaks

1/4 teaspoon salt

1-1/2 teaspoons coarsely ground black pepper

3 tablespoons margarine or butter, divided

2 tablespoons olive oil

1/2 cup minced Vidalia onion

1 garlic clove, minced

1/2 cup red wine

1 cup mushrooms, thinly sliced

1/2 cup heavy cream (skim milk can be used)

1 medium tomato, peeled and coarsely chopped

4 large fresh basil leaves, chopped

Pat steaks dry. Rub salt and pepper onto both sides of each steak. In a large, heavy skillet, melt 2 tablespoons margarine and oil over high heat. Add the steaks and cook until browned and to desired doneness. Transfer the steaks to a warmed dish and loosely cover with foil to keep warm.

Add remaining 1 tablespoon margarine to the skillet. Add the onion and garlic and sauté 1 minute. Add wine to the skillet and bring to a boil over high heat, stirring to scrape up any browned bits. Add the mushrooms and cook, stirring frequently until softened, about 3 minutes. Add the cream, tomato and basil and simmer until the mixture begins to thicken (about 1 minute). Season with additional salt and pepper to taste. Spoon sauce over the steaks and serve.

Serves 4

Venison Philly Sandwich

3/4 pound venison loin, cut
    into thin strips
Italian salad dressing
3 tablespoons margarine
Several slices sweet onion
4-5 mushrooms
Bread and cheese of your
    choice

Place sliced venison in a bowl and cover with Italian dressing. Marinate for about 30 minutes. Melt the margarine in a small frying pan; sauté onion and mushrooms until tender. Drain venison and add to onion/mushroom mixture. Cook about 2 minutes or until loin is still slightly pink. Meanwhile, place sliced bread and cheese under the broiler to melt cheese. Top with loin mixture and serve immediately open-face style.

Serves 1

Honey and Mustard Steaks with Onion Mushroom Wine Sauce

1 pound cubed venison steaks

Honey and Mustard Sauce:

1/3 cup stone-ground mustard with horseradish (or your favorite Dijon-style mustard)
1 teaspoon Italian seasonings
2 tablespoons honey
1 tablespoon cider vinegar
1 tablespoon water
2 tablespoons wine
1/8 teaspoon coarsely ground black pepper

Onion Mushroom Wine Sauce:

2 tablespoons olive oil
1 small onion, sliced
1 cup sliced mushrooms
2 tablespoons sugar
1/4 cup wine

Combine mustard sauce ingredients. Place cubed steaks in grilling pan (or non-stick frying pan) and brush both sides with mustard sauce. Grill 8 - 10 minutes, turning steaks and brushing with honey mustard sauce.

Meanwhile, prepare Onion Mushroom Wine Sauce. Place olive oil in small frying pan and heat. Add onions, mushrooms and sugar and sauté briefly. Add wine and continue to cook until wine is reduced by half. Pour over Honey Mustard Cubed Steaks and serve immediately.

Stuffed Venison

1 boned venison rump roast, or
  rolled roast
1 cup Italian salad dressing
1 pound bulk pork sausage
Salt and pepper

Cover roast in Italian dressing and marinate in the refrigerator 4 - 8 hours. Drain and place pork sausage inside roast and roll. Tie or secure with toothpicks. Wrap in foil, place in roasting pan and bake at 400 degrees until done. Use your meat thermometer to check on doneness.

Tip: A tenderloin is nice prepared in this manner. Try serving one loin stuffed with shrimp (see recipe on page 62) and one with sausage. The loin takes only about 1/2 pound sausage.

Shrimp-Stuffed Tenderloin with Wine Sauce

1 whole venison tenderloin
1/2 - 1 cup Italian salad
  dressing
12 whole shrimp, cooked and
  peeled
1 tablespoon butter, melted
2 teaspoons lemon juice
1 - 2 slices bacon

Wine Sauce:

1/2 cup butter (no substitution)
1/4 cup finely chopped onion
1/2 cup sliced mushrooms
1 - 2 large garlic cloves, minced
1/2 cup white wine
1/2 teaspoon Worcestershire
  sauce

Cut loin lengthwise to within 1/4 – 1/2 inch of bottom to butterfly. Place loin in Italian dressing to marinate for at least 4 hours. Cook shrimp in water seasoned with Old Bay and peel. Place shrimp end to end inside loin. Melt butter in a microwave and add lemon juice; drizzle over shrimp. Close meat around shrimp and secure with toothpicks (or string). Place bacon strips along the cut where the shrimp were inserted and secure with toothpicks. Place loin on a rack in broiler pan and roast at 400 degrees for about 40 minutes or until loin is medium rare. (An instant-read meat thermometer is very helpful here.)

Meanwhile, prepare wine sauce. Melt butter. Sauté onion, mushrooms and garlic until tender. Add wine and Worcestershire sauce and simmer slowly to reduce to about half. To serve, slice loin, remove toothpicks, and spoon on wine sauce.

Tips: Serve with baked brown rice and baked apricots; both can be placed in the oven while the roast cooks. Add a green salad and you have a delicious meal.

Basil Venison

1 pound cubed venison steaks, cut into thin strips

Italian salad dressing

Fresh vegetables of your choice, such as onion, yellow squash, zucchini, carrots, sugar snap peas

Basil Butter:

2 ounces fresh basil (2 bunches)

10 ounces butter or margarine

1 large garlic clove, minced

1/8 teaspoon black pepper

4 tablespoons Parmesan cheese, grated

Place strips of steak in a non-metal container and cover with Italian salad dressing. Marinate at least 30 minutes but 3 - 4 hours is better. Slice or chop mixed fresh vegetables of your choice: onion, yellow squash, zucchini, carrots, sugar snap peas (if frozen, defrost).

Prepare basil butter. Remove large stems from basil and wash. Shake off excess water and dry. Place basil in a food processor. Add other ingredients and pulse until basil is chopped and all the ingredients are mixed well. Store in the refrigerator and use as needed. Keeps for 7 days.

Cook vegetables in basil butter until partially done. Drain venison and add to vegetables. Continue cooking until venison is done. Serve immediately over rice.

Tip: Try this basil butter with pasta and shrimp; it is delicious.

Bourbon Mustard Steak

1 pound cubed venison steaks
Salt and pepper to taste
2 tablespoons mustard, such as
  Grey Poupon
2 tablespoons margarine
2 tablespoons olive oil
2 green onions, chopped
2 tablespoons bourbon
1 can (4 ounces) mushrooms,
  drained
1/4 teaspoon dried chives
1/4 teaspoon dried parsley
1/4 teaspoon dried Italian
  seasoning
4 tablespoons sour cream

Season steaks with salt and pepper and spread mustard generously on both sides of steaks. Melt margarine and add olive oil in skillet. Brown steaks quickly on medium-high heat until desired doneness is reached. Do not overcook. Remove steaks. Add green onions and sauté. Add bourbon and cook until most of the liquid evaporates. Add mushrooms, herbs and sour cream, blending thoroughly with pan juices. Pour over steaks and serve with rice.

Chive Steaks

1 pound cubed venison steaks

Chive Butter:

1/4 cup butter (or margarine) at room temperature
2 - 3 tablespoons fresh chives, chopped
2 teaspoons freshly squeezed lemon juice
1/2 teaspoon salt
1/4 teaspoon black pepper

In a small bowl combine the butter, chives, lemon juice, salt and pepper. Using a fork, mix vigorously until blended. Place about half the butter in a sauté pan over medium-high heat. Add steaks and cook quickly to desired doneness. Just before removing from the pan, place a bit of butter on each steak and allow it to melt before removing steaks. Serve immediately.

Serves 4

Tip: Try broiled tomatoes with the steaks.

Crab-Stuffed Venison Steak Rolls

Stuffing:

1/4 – 1/2 stick margarine or
  butter
1 garlic clove, minced
1/4 cup chopped celery
1/4 cup chopped onion
1/2 pound imitation crab, cut
  into small chunks (or real
  crab)
1 tablespoon dried parsley
1/2 teaspoon dried cilantro
Salt and pepper to taste

Steaks and Wine Sauce:

2 tablespoons margarine or
  butter
1 garlic clove, minced
4 venison cubed steaks (flatten
  if necessary)
4 large slices onion
1 cup zinfandel wine
1/2 cup sour cream
Salt and pepper to taste

To prepare stuffing, melt margarine in a skillet and add garlic, celery and onion. Sauté vegetables until soft. Add crab, herbs, salt and pepper. Remove from the pan.

Add 2 tablespoons margarine to the pan and lightly cook garlic; add steaks and quickly brown on both sides. Remove from pan and let cool enough to handle. Place stuffing in the center of steaks and roll. Secure with as many toothpicks as needed. Cut 4 large slices of onion and place in the pan. Place steak rolls on top of each onion slice. Pour wine over steaks. Cover and simmer 15 - 20 minutes or until tender. Carefully remove onion and steak roll from pan and place on a dish. Add 1/2 cup sour cream to pan drippings and cook, stirring constantly, until warm but not boiling. Salt and pepper to taste. Pour over steaks and serve immediately.

Venison and Paprika

1/3 cup margarine
1 large onion, chopped
2 garlic cloves, minced
2 pounds boneless venison
    stew meat, cut into 1/2-inch
    cubes
1 tablespoon paprika
1 teaspoon salt
1/4 teaspoon black pepper
1/2 cup water
2 tablespoons flour
1 cup sour cream

Melt margarine in Dutch oven. Add onion and garlic. Cook until tender but not brown. Remove from pan and set aside. Brown meat in remaining margarine over moderate heat. Add paprika to meat and margarine and stir about 1 minute. Return onion and garlic to pan; add salt, pepper and water. Cover and simmer 1-1/2 to 2 hours. Add more water if necessary. Combine flour and sour cream and stir into meat mixture and cook until smooth and thickened. Do not boil. Serve with pasta.

Serves 6

Venison Strips with Mushroom Sauce

1 pound venison sirloin steak
Flour - about 1/2 cup
3 tablespoons olive oil
1/2 cup chopped onion
1 cup mushrooms
1 cup water
Several dashes Worcestershire
   sauce
Salt and black pepper to taste

Place steak on a floured cutting board, pound meat with meat tenderizer (or side of a saucer) until thin; add flour as needed and do not allow to get gummy. Pound and flour both sides of steaks. Cut steaks into 1/2-inch strips.

Heat olive oil in a large frying pan. Add steak strips and quickly brown (2 - 3 minutes). Steaks brown better if not crowded in pan. Remove from pan. Add onion and mushrooms and sauté until tender. Add 2 tablespoons flour and cook for 1 minute. Add 1 cup water, several dashes of Worcestershire sauce, salt and pepper and bring to a boil to thicken. Return steak strips to pan with sauce to reheat. Serve over hot biscuits or rice.

Stroganoff with Tomatoes

1-1/2 pounds venison sirloin
   steak, cut into 1/4-inch slices
2 teaspooons fresh thyme
4 tablespoons olive oil

Sauce:

1 large onion, thinly sliced
1/2 pound mushrooms, sliced
2 garlic cloves, minced
2 tablespoons all-purpose flour
1 can (14 ounces) diced
   tomatoes in juice
1/2 cup beef broth
1/8 teaspoon cayenne pepper
Freshly ground black pepper to
   taste

Sprinkle venison with salt, thyme and black pepper. Heat 2 tablespoons olive oil in a heavy, deep skillet over medium-high heat. Add half of meat and cook until browned, about 2 minutes. Remove meat from pan; repeat with remaining meat.

In same skillet, sauté onion (add 1 tablespoon oil if needed) over medium-high heat until brown, about 8 minutes. Transfer onion to browned meat. Sauté mushrooms and garlic (adding 1 tablespoon oil if necessary) until tender. Cook until liquid from mushrooms evaporates. Sprinkle with 2 tablespoons flour and stir 1 minute. Return meat and onions with accumulated juices to skillet. Add undrained tomatoes, broth and cayenne; bring to a boil. Reduce heat and simmer until venison is tender. Serve over egg noodles or pasta. Garnish with parsley.

Serves 4 - 6

Cubed Steak Italiano

2 tablespoons olive oil
1 pound cubed venison steaks,
  cut into strips
1 onion, sliced
1 green pepper, cut into strips
1 garlic clove, minced
1 cup sliced mushrooms
1 jar meatless spaghetti sauce
1 teaspoon dried basil
Salt and pepper to taste

In a large skillet, heat olive oil and sauté steak strips, onion, green pepper, garlic and mushrooms until done. Stir in spaghetti sauce, basil, salt and pepper. Cover and simmer for 15 - 30 minutes to blend flavors. Serve over pasta of your choice.

Serves 4

Orange Cubed Steaks

1 pound venison cubed steaks
2 tablespoons olive oil
1 large onion, thinly sliced
1/2 teaspoon freshly grated
   orange zest
2 garlic cloves, minced
1/2 cup low-salt beef broth
2 teaspoons soy sauce

Pat steaks dry between paper towels (to prevent oil from popping) and season with salt and pepper. In a heavy skillet, heat oil over moderately high heat until hot (but not smoking) and brown steaks. Transfer steaks to a plate and in drippings remaining in skillet, cook onion over moderate heat until tender. Stir in zest and garlic and cook until fragrant, about 30 seconds. Add broth, soy sauce, and steaks and simmer until steaks are tender. Serve over orange couscous.

Serves 3 - 4

Tip: Orange-glazed asparagus compliments this dish. Place 1-1/2 pounds asparagus in a skillet (with a lid). Add 1/2 teaspoon salt, 1 teaspoon olive oil, and 1/2 cup orange juice. Cook, covered, until asparagus is tender crisp. Remove asparagus from pan. Add zest of an orange to pan sauce and cook until sauce is reduced to a glaze. Pour over asparagus and serve.

Oven-Cooked Country-Style Steak

1-1/2 to 2 pounds venison
  cubed steak
1/2 cup all-purpose flour
1/4 teaspoon salt
1/2 teaspoon black pepper
1 can (10.75 ounces) cream of
  mushroom soup
1 can (10.75 ounces) bouillon
  (or use bouillon cubes
  dissolved in hot water)

Season flour with salt and pepper. Flour steaks and place in a foil-lined Dutch oven. Heat mushroom soup and bouillon, stirring to mix well. Pour over meat. Bring foil over steaks to cover well. Bake in a 350-degree oven for 1 hour or until tender.

Tip: Use 2 bouillon cubes and 2 cans of water if using more meat; you do not need to add an additional can of mushroom soup.

Easy Pizza Venison Swiss Steak

1 pound venison cubed steak
1/3 cup all-purpose flour
1/2 teaspoon salt
1/4 teaspoon black pepper
3 tablespoons olive oil
1 onion, sliced
1 cup fresh mushrooms, sliced
1 jar (15 ounces) pizza sauce
1/4 cup water
1 bay leaf
1/4 teaspoon oregano
1/4 teaspoon basil
1/4 teaspoon Italian seasoning
1/2 - 1 cup shredded
    mozzarella cheese

Combine flour, salt and pepper. Dredge steaks in flour mixture. Brown steaks, in batches, in hot oil in a large skillet over high heat, 1 - 2 minutes on each side. Remove steaks and place in a lightly greased 9 x 13-inch baking dish.

Sauté onion and mushrooms in skillet over medium heat until tender. Add pizza sauce, rinsing jar with water. Add herbs and spices. Bring to a boil and pour over steak. Bake, covered, at 350 degrees for 45 minutes. Uncover and sprinkle with cheese. Return to oven until cheese melts. Serve with pasta, salad and Texas toast.

Serves 4 - 6

Garlic Loin Toast Appetizers

Loin:

2 garlic cloves, minced
1/2 teaspoon kosher salt
1 tablespoon olive oil
1/4 teaspoon dried oregano
1/4 teaspoon freshly ground
  black pepper
Dash ground red pepper
10-12 ounces venison loin,
  unsliced

Tapenade:

2 tablespoons chopped
  sun-dried tomatoes packed
  in oil, drained
1 tablespoon chopped
  kalamata olives
1 teaspoon chopped fresh
  oregano
2 teaspoons chopped capers
1 teaspoon Worcestershire
  sauce
1 teaspoon olive oil

French bread baguette

For rub, place salt on a cutting board and chop garlic in salt. Using the back of a fork, mash garlic with salt to form a paste. Blend paste together with oil, oregano, black and red peppers. Rub over loin, refrigerate and marinate for 1 - 2 hours.

Grill or broil loin until desired doneness is reached (an instant read thermometer is handy here). Do not overcook. Remove from grill and let rest 10 minutes. Slice loin thinly.

For tapenade, finely chop sun-dried tomatoes, olives, oregano and capers. Combine with Worcestershire sauce and olive oil. Cover and refrigerate until ready to serve.

To assemble appetizers, place a dollop of tapenade on sliced French bread baguette toast or garlic toast and top with thinly sliced venison loin.

Tips: The loin can be served hot or cold. These are delicious as appetizers but are also good for picnics, tailgating or pot luck socials. This tapenade compliments the venison, but there are lots of interesting tapenades widely available at grocery stores.

Venison and Pepperoncini Bites

Venison slices, 1/4-inch thick
Italian salad dressing
Bacon slices, cut in half and
pre-cooked a bit in the
microwave

Marinate venison slices in your favorite oil and vinegar dressing (we like Paul Newman's Olive Oil and Vinegar) for at least 4 hours.

Wrap venison slices around pepperoncini and then wrap a half strip of bacon around each venison/pepper package and secure with a toothpick. Place on a hot grill and cook approximately 5 - 8 minutes or until venison is medium rare and bacon has completed cooking.

Tips: Optional stuffings for variations: water chestnuts, pepper cheese, or jalapeño pepper half and onion slice. Dove breasts are delicious prepared in the same manner.

Sweet and Sour Venison Appetizers

1 stick margarine, melted
1 cup vinegar
1 teaspoon Worcestershire
  sauce
1/4 – 1/2 teaspoon black
  pepper
Salt to taste
1 pound venison steak, cut into
  bite-size chunks

Combine melted margarine, vinegar, Worcestershire sauce, pepper and salt. Marinate steak bits 15 - 30 minutes and drain well. Place on a medium-hot grill and cook until bites are medium rare. Do not overcook. Serve with apricot sauce for dipping.

Apricot Sauce:

1 cup apricot preserves
1/4 cup freshly squeezed
  lemon juice
1/4 cup water
2 teaspoons cornstarch
1 tablespoon brown sugar
2 tablespoons brandy

Mix all ingredients except brandy in a small sauce pan. Stir to blend and cook until slightly thickened. Remove from heat, add brandy and continue to cook until thickened. Serve with venison bites.

Makes 1-1/2 cups

Tips: A perforated grill pan or wok makes an easy task of grilling the bites that could easily fall through the grate. These pans are inexpensive and a great tool for the grill lover. Dove breasts can be prepared in the same manner. This sauce goes well with other red meats such as duck or goose.

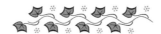

Creole Venison Bits

3/4 - 1 pound venison steak, cut
  into small chunks
1/2 - 1 stick butter
Creole seasoning

Melt butter in a large frying pan over medium heat and quickly sauté steak bits in butter. Sprinkle with Creole seasoning as you cook the bits. Venison should be cooked to medium rare; venison is best if still pink inside. Serve immediately.

Tips: These are delicious as an appetizer. You will find you cannot cook them fast enough for your guests! Try dove breast fillets like this also.

Venison Steak Fingers

1 pound venison steak, cut into strips

Marinade:

1/2 cup olive oil
1/4 cup wine (red or white)
1 teaspoon dried basil
1/2 teaspoon Montreal Steak Seasoning
1 sleeve plain saltine crackers, crumbled
Olive oil

Place steak strips in a resealable plastic bag and top with marinade ingredients, mixing well. Refrigerate and marinate for 4 hours.

Heat olive oil (enough to cover the bottom of your pan) in a frying pan. Dip steak (wet – do not pat dry) in cracker crumbs and sauté in hot olive oil until golden brown on both sides and pink (medium rare) in the center. Serve with mustard sauce of your choice.

Honey Mustard Sauce:

1/3 cup honey
1-1/2 cups mayonnaise
1/4 teaspoon freshly ground black pepper
Dash of Worcestershire sauce
1-1/2 tablespoons mustard
1/8 teaspoon kosher salt
3/4 teaspoon dried cilantro

Mix ingredients well and store in refrigerator.

Creole Mustard Sauce:

1 container (8 ounces) sour cream
1/4 cup Creole mustard
1 tablespoon cider vinegar
1 teaspoon Cajun seasoning
Several dashes hot pepper sauce

Mix all ingredients together and refrigerate.

Tips: Try the steak fingers as hors d'oeuvres. The honey mustard sauce is delicious as a salad or fruit dressing.

Oven Roasted Ribs

1 venison rib rack

Dry Spice Rub:

1 tablespoon chili powder
1 teaspoon ground cumin
1/2 teaspoon dried cilantro
   leaves
1-1/2 teaspoons coarse kosher
   salt
1-1/2 teaspoons paprika
1/2 tablespoon dark brown
   sugar
1/2 teaspoon black pepper
1/8 teaspoon cayenne pepper

Stir spices together in a small bowl. Preheat oven to 300 degrees. Sprinkle and press rub into both sides of rib rack. Place ribs on broiler pan rack (sprayed with Pam) meaty side up. Lightly sprinkle with additional salt. Rotate pan after first hour and every 30 minutes thereafter until tender, usually about 2 to 2-1/2 hours. Slice into individual ribs and serve with your favorite barbecue sauce for dipping. Although the rub gives good flavor, the ribs are dry without the dipping sauce.

Serves 2

Tip: For meatier ribs, leave the backstraps in place and saw down the middle of the spine. Ribs are often discarded, but there is meat there to be utilized.

Chapter 4

Simple and Scrumptious: Using Ground Venison

One of the beauties of ground venison is that many of the pieces of the deer commonly discarded can be used in this fashion. Neck meat, the ribs and flanks, and indeed all edible portions except organ meats can be turned into ground meat. It is advisable, in most situations, to "adulterate" the venison a bit with the addition of some fat. Most processors do this as a matter of course, although we recommend that you specify the addition of only 10 percent or so of beef suet. If you don't want any fat, fine, but when this is the case, you will need to take some steps to keep burgers from crumbling or use a bit of oil when browning the meat.

Many of the dishes that follow might be described as ethnic in nature. You will find, for example, a lot of recipes that feature foods we associate with Italy. Many of these, when accompanied by crusty bread laced with garlic, a good salad and a glass of red wine, will remind you of why the Italians attach so much importance to meals and leisurely dining. Yet that's not all by any means. There are also recipes that harken back to Greece, central Europe, England and the spicy, satisfying fare we normally describe as Tex-Mex.

While both of us certainly enjoy international dining as done through the medium of venison, there's absolutely nothing wrong with being as country as cornbread and as American as a burger (sure, there's a substitution there supplanting apple pie, but to us it seems quite appropriate). With the cuisine of our own country in mind, we wrap up this chapter with a burger extravaganza. Venison makes wonderful burgers – lean, luscious and far healthier than the sort of fat-laced ones you find in fast-food emporiums. We think you will find the double dozen – 12 sauces for burgers plus 12 ways to jazz them up – a pair of culinary windows that opens up on a whole new world of burgers.

Venison Meatball Lasagna

Meatballs:

1 to 1-1/2 pounds ground
  venison
1/4 cup finely minced onion
1 garlic clove, finely minced
1/2 cup quick-cooking oats,
  uncooked
1 egg, lightly beaten
1/2 cup milk
1/2 teaspoon kosher salt
1 teaspoon dried Italian
  seasoning
1/4 teaspoon black pepper

1/3 cup flour
1 teaspoon paprika

Combine first 9 ingredients. Mix gently and shape into 1-inch balls. Chill meatballs for at least 30 minutes.

Mix flour and paprika; gently roll meatballs in flour mixture and place on a lightly greased rack in a 9 x 13-inch pan.

Bake at 400 degrees for 25-30 minutes. Drain on paper towels, if needed.

Lasagna:

1 container (15 ounces) ricotta
  cheese
1 container (8 ounces) soft
  onion and chive cream
  cheese
1 teaspoon dried basil
1/2 teaspoon garlic salt
1/4 teaspoon black pepper

3 cups shredded mozzarella
  cheese, divided
1-1/2 cups shredded Parmesan
  cheese, divided
2 jars (26 ounces each) tomato-
  basil pasta sauce, divided
1 package (9 ounces) no boil
  lasagna noodles
50-60 cooked venison
  meatballs

Stir together first 5 ingredients until blended. Stir in 1/2 cup mozzarella cheese and 1/2 cup Parmesan cheese; set aside.

Spread 1 cup pasta sauce in bottom of a lightly greased 9 x 13-inch baking dish. Place 4 lasagna noodles over pasta sauce. Top with meatballs. Spoon 3 cups pasta sauce over meatballs; sprinkle with 3/4 cup mozzarella cheese. Arrange 4 more noodles evenly over mozzarella cheese. Spread ricotta cheese mixture evenly over noodles. Top with 4 more noodles and pasta sauce.

Bake, covered, at 350 degrees for 1 hour. Top with remaining mozzarella cheese and Parmesan

Venison Meatball Lasagna *(cont.)*

cheese. Bake, uncovered, 15 more minutes or until cheese melts and is slightly browned. Let stand for 15-20 minutes before serving.

Serves 8 - 10

Tips: These baked meatballs are quite versatile. It is handy to keep several batches in the freezer. To freeze, cool completely and seal in an airtight container. Use in lasagna, pasta sauce with spaghetti, meatball subs or as an appetizer with your favorite sauce.

Meatball Subs
with Quick Marinara Sauce

Meatballs:

1 pound ground venison
1 egg, slightly beaten
1/3 cup finely diced onion
1/4 cup Italian bread crumbs
2 garlic cloves, minced
1/4 teaspoon crushed red
   pepper flakes
2 teaspoon Worcestershire
   sauce
1 teaspoon dried parsley
1 teaspoon dried oregano
1 teaspoon Montreal Steak
   Seasoning
1/3 cup shredded Parmesan
   cheese

Marinara Sauce:

2 tablespoons olive oil
2 garlic cloves, minced
1/3 cup chopped onion
1/4 teaspoon crushed red
   pepper flakes
1 can (28 ounces) crushed
   tomatoes
2 teaspoons dried Italian
   seasoning
1/2 teaspoon dried basil
Salt to taste

4 - 6 crusty sub rolls

Place ground venison in a large mixing bowl and make a well in the center. Add all the other meatball ingredients into the well. Gently mix the meatballs until well combined; however, do not over mix. Shape into balls (using a heaping tablespoon per meatball) and place on a greased baking sheet. Bake in a 375 degree oven for 20 minutes or until meat is cooked through.

Meanwhile, prepare marinara sauce. Heat 2 tablespoons olive oil in a sauce pan over medium heat. Add onion and sauté until tender. Add garlic and red pepper flakes and sauté briefly (about 30 seconds) until garlic sizzles. Stir in the tomatoes, herbs and seasonings. Bring to a slight bubble and simmer until meatballs are removed from oven.

Place meatballs in sub rolls and pour sauce over them. Serve immediately.

Serves 4 - 6

Tips: Crushed cornflakes can be substituted for the Italian bread crumbs. Top subs with shredded cheese and place under the broiler to melt cheese.

Quick and Easy Calzones

1 tablespoon olive oil
1/2 cup minced onion
1/2 cup mushrooms, sliced
2 garlic cloves, minced
1/2 pound ground venison
1 jar (14 ounces) chunky
    spaghetti sauce
1/2 teaspoon dried Italian
    seasoning
1 can (11 ounces) refrigerated
    French bread loaf
3 slices mozzarella cheese

Heat olive oil in nonstick skillet over medium heat. Sauté onions and mushrooms until tender; add garlic and sauté about 1 minute. Combine ground venison with onion/mushroom mixture and cook until meat is no longer pink. If needed, drain well and return mixture to skillet; stir in 1/3 cup spaghetti sauce and Italian seasoning.

Unroll French loaf and roll into a 14-inch square (or as close as possible). Cut into 3 squares; spoon 1/3 of venison mixture into center of each square. Top each with a slice of mozzarella cheese. Fold over to form a triangle, pressing edges to seal. Place on a lightly greased baking sheet. Bake at 400 degrees for 15 minutes or until browned. Serve with remaining spaghetti sauce, which has been heated.

Serves 3

Tips: The most challenging part of this recipe is rolling out the French loaf. Flour both the work surface and rolling pin and be patient. Brush the edges with beaten egg white for "glue" to make them seal better. After sealed, brush top of calzones with egg white and sprinkle with kosher (coarse) salt.

Pizza Dip

1/2 pound ground venison
1 jar (14 ounces) pizza sauce
4 ounces grated cheddar cheese
4 ounces grated mozzarella
cheese
1/2 teaspoon dried oregano
1-1/2 teaspoons cornstarch
1/2 cup Parmesan cheese

In a skillet, brown venison and stir to crumble finely. Combine all ingredients except Parmesan cheese in a slow cooker. Cover and heat on low 2 - 3 hours. After 1 hour, sprinkle Parmesan cheese on top.

Serve with pita toasts or tortilla chips for dipping.

Tip: To make pita toasts, cut pita bread into triangles and divide them into single pieces. Toast briefly in a 400-degree oven and serve with pizza dip.

Italian-Style Sloppy Joes

1 tablespoon olive oil
1/3 cup finely chopped onion
1 garlic clove, minced
1/2 pound ground venison
1/4 cup tomato sauce
1/4 cup ketchup
2 tablespoons Parmesan cheese
1/2 teaspoon dried Italian
seasoning
Salt and black pepper to taste

4 slices mozzarella cheese
4 hamburger buns

Preheat oven to 350 degrees.
In a medium, non-stick skillet, heat 1 tablespoon olive oil. Add chopped onions and cook until tender; add garlic and cook until garlic is fragrant (about 30 seconds). Add ground venison and sauté until meat is browned; combine tomato sauce, ketchup, Parmesan cheese, Italian seasoning, salt and pepper with meat and sauté to blend and heat through. Place on hamburger buns and top with mozzarella cheese. Wrap in foil and seal. Bake in 350-degree oven for 15 minutes. Serve immediately.

Serves 4

Spicy Venison and Black Olive Rotini

2 tablespoons extra-virgin olive oil
1/2 cup chopped onion
2 garlic cloves, minced
1/8 - 1/4 teaspoon crushed red chile pepper flakes
1/2 pound ground venison
1/8 teaspoon ground cinnamon (or a little less)
Kosher salt
Freshly ground black pepper
1 can (14 ounces) diced tomatoes
1/3 pound dried rotini pasta
1/4 teaspoon granulated sugar
1/4 cup pitted black olives, quartered lengthwise
1 tablespoon dried parsley
Parmesan cheese

Put a large pot of water on to boil for the pasta.

Heat the olive oil in a large skillet over medium heat. Add onion and cook until tender. Add garlic and pepper flakes. When the garlic is fragrant (but not browned), about 1 minute, add venison and cinnamon. Season generously with black pepper and salt to taste. Use a large spoon to break up the venison into small pieces.

Salt the water after it boils and add pasta.

Pour the tomatoes and juice into the skillet with venison, reduce the heat to medium low and cook for 8 - 10 minutes. Stir in the sugar, olives, and parsley. Taste and adjust salt and pepper if needed.

Drain rotini when it is tender and add to the meat sauce; mix well for about 1 minute. Serve immediately and top with additional parsley and Parmesan cheese.

Serves 2 - 3

Tip: This is a different combination of flavors, but the spicy from the red and black peppers and sweet from the cinnamon compliment the venison and make a quick and easy meal.

Ziti with Venison, Sausage and Cannellini

1/2 pound ground venison
1/2 pound bulk pork sausage
2 tablespoons olive oil, divided
1 medium onion, chopped
2 cloves garlic, minced
Dash of red pepper flakes
1 can (14 ounces) diced
   tomatoes
1 can (8 ounces) tomato sauce
1 cup water from cooking pasta
1 can (15 ounces) cannellini
   (white kidney beans) beans,
   rinsed and drained
15 fresh basil leaves, roughly
   cut
1/4 – 1/2 teaspoon kosher salt
1/4 teaspoon freshly ground
   black pepper
1/2 pound ziti, cooked

Heat 1 tablespoon olive oil in a large skillet, and sauté venison and sausage (breaking it up as it cooks) over medium-high heat. Remove from pan and drain well. Return the pan to heat and add second tablespoon olive oil. Reduce heat to medium and add onion. Cook for 5 minutes. Add garlic and red pepper flakes, stirring constantly for 1 minute. Add tomatoes, tomato sauce, pasta water, beans, basil, salt and pepper. Heat through. Return meats to sauce. Drain pasta and combine with sauce. Serve with grated Parmesan cheese and garlic bread.

Serves 6

Tip: One would not normally think of combining pasta and beans, but their union in this dish provides a pleasant surprise.

Swift and Simple Garlic Meat Sauce

1 tablespoon olive oil
1/2 large onion, chopped
1 pound ground venison
Cracked black pepper to taste
4 garlic cloves, minced
1/4 teaspoon crushed red
    pepper flakes
1/4 teaspoon allspice (do not
    omit)
1 cup canned beef broth
1/3 cup red wine
1 can (28 ounces) crushed
    tomatoes
2 tablespoons chopped fresh
    parsley
2 tablespoons chopped fresh
    oregano
Grated Parmesan cheese

Heat olive oil over medium-high heat in a large skillet and sauté chopped onion until tender. Add ground venison seasoned with black pepper and cook until browned. Add garlic, crushed red pepper and allspice and cook about 1 minute. Add broth and red wine and stir to remove browned bits from the bottom of the pan. Add tomatoes, parsley and oregano. Reduce heat and simmer while you cook the pasta. Toss with pasta and top with grated cheese. Serve with bread and a green salad.

Serves 4

Tip: Use more crushed red pepper flakes if you like more heat in your sauce. Allspice is the secret ingredient; you will be pleasantly surprised at the difference it makes.

Spaghetti and Meatballs

Sauce:

1/4 cup chopped onion
2 garlic cloves, minced
1 tablespoon olive oil
1-1/2 cups water
1 can (16 ounces) tomato sauce
1 can (12 ounces) tomato paste
1/4 cup minced fresh parsley
1/2 tablespoon dried basil
1/2 tablespoon dried oregano
1 teaspoon salt
1/4 teaspoon black pepper

Meatballs:

1-1/2 pounds ground venison
2 eggs, lightly beaten
1 cup soft bread crumbs
   (use a blender to make fine
   crumbs)
3/4 cups milk
1/2 cup grated Parmesan
   cheese
2 garlic cloves, minced
1 teaspoon salt
1/2 teaspoon black pepper

For the sauce: In a Dutch oven over medium heat, sauté onion and garlic in oil. Add water, tomato sauce and paste, parsley, basil, oregano, salt and pepper; bring to a boil. Reduce heat; cover and simmer for about 1 hour.

For the meatballs: Combine meatball ingredients and mix well. Shape into 1 1/2-inch balls. Place meatballs on a cookie sheet and refrigerate several hours (or in the freezer for 15 - 20 minutes). Place 2 tablespoons olive oil in a large skillet over medium heat and add meatballs. Brown meatballs on all sides and add to sauce. Simmer for about 30 minutes, gently stirring occasionally. Be very gentle with your stirring to keep from tearing up the meatballs. Serve over spaghetti.

Serves 6

Tip: Chilling is the secret to keeping the meatballs whole.

Herbed Meat Sauce

1 tablespoon olive oil
1 medium onion, chopped
2 -3 garlic cloves, minced
1 pound ground venison
1/2 pound Italian sausage,
   removed from casings
1 can (14 ounces) tomatoes
1 can (14 ounces) diced
   tomatoes
1 can (8 ounces) tomato sauce
3/4 cup water
1 teaspoon sugar
1/2 teaspoon salt
1/2 cup fresh basil and oregano
   (chopped and packed)
1/8 teaspoon black pepper
1 pound spaghetti, cooked
Freshly grated Parmesan
   cheese

Heat olive oil in a large, deep skillet over medium heat. Add onion and garlic and cook until onions are translucent. Add venison and sausage and cook until meat is no longer pink. Add remaining ingredients and bring to a boil, reduce heat and simmer (covered) for 1 hour or until sauce thickens slightly. Add sauce to drained pasta and top with freshly grated Parmesan cheese.

Serves 6

Tip: This is a low-cost meal. The sauce freezes well.

Ziti

1 pound ground venison

1/4 – 1/2 pound bulk venison
sausage

1/2 cup chopped onions

2 garlic cloves, minced

3-1/2 cups meatless spaghetti
sauce

1 cup chicken broth

1 tablespoon chopped fresh
oregano

1 tablespoon chopped fresh
parsley

16 ounces ziti, cooked and
drained

2 cups shredded mozzarella
cheese, divided

1 cup grated Parmesan cheese,
divided

In a large skillet over medium-high heat, sauté ground venison, sausage, onions and garlic 6 - 8 minutes until venison is browned. Stir in spaghetti sauce, chicken broth, oregano and parsley. Reduce heat; simmer 10 - 15 minutes. Stir 1 cup of sauce into cooked ziti. Spoon half the ziti mixture into 9 x 13-inch baking dish. Sprinkle with 1-1/2 cups mozzarella and 1/2 cup Parmesan. Top with 2 cups sauce, then remaining ziti mixture and sauce. Cover and bake in a 350-degree oven for 20 minutes. Sprinkle with remaining mozzarella and Parmesan. Bake uncovered 10 minutes longer or until heated through, cheese has melted and ziti is bubbly.

Serves 8

Tip: Try adding a cup of ricotta cheese in the center with the mozzarella and Parmesan.

Speedy Meat Sauce

1-1/2 pounds ground venison
1/2 cup chopped onion
2 garlic cloves, minced
2 tablespoons olive oil
1 can (14 ounces) stewed
   tomatoes, cut up
1 can (6 ounces) V-8 or tomato
   juice
1 jar (14 ounces) Classico or
   Prego meatless spaghetti
   sauce
1 teaspoon grape jelly
1/2 teaspoon dried oregano
1/2 teaspoon dried basil

Brown meat in olive oil along with the onion and garlic. Stir in other ingredients. Cook 15 - 20 minutes or until jelly melts. Serve over pasta.

Serves 6 - 8

Simple Spaghetti Sauce

3 tablespoons olive oil
1 medium onion, chopped
4 garlic cloves, minced
1 pound fresh mushrooms,
  sliced
1 pound bulk venison sausage
1 pound ground venison
2 cans (16 ounces each) diced
  tomatoes
2 cans (6 ounces each) tomato
  paste
2 tablespoons minced fresh
  parsley
1-1/2 teaspoons dried oregano
1 teaspoon salt
1/2 teaspoon black pepper (or
  to taste)
1 cup red wine
  (such as merlot)

Heat 3 tablespoons oil in a Dutch oven and sauté onion, garlic and mushrooms. Brown sausage and ground venison; add to vegetables. Add remaining ingredients; cover and simmer for about 2 hours or until sauce has thickened and flavors have blended. Serve over pasta.

Serves 6 - 8

Tip: If you like a hot and spicy sauce, try adding 1 - 2 tablespoons canned jalapeno peppers (along with some of the juice) to the sauce.

Cranberry Meatballs

Meatballs:

1-1/2 pounds ground venison
1/2 cup oats, regular or quick
   cooking (not instant)
1/2 cup milk
1 egg, beaten
1/4 cup onion, finely minced
1 garlic clove, finely minced
1/4 teaspoon black pepper
1/2 - 1 teaspoon salt
1 tablespoon dried parsley
   flakes

Sauce:

8 ounces whole berry
   cranberry sauce (1/2 can)
1 jar (12 ounces) chili sauce
1 tablespoon brown sugar
1 tablespoon lemon juice
1 tablespoon orange juice

For meatballs: Combine all ingredients and mix well. Form into 1-inch balls. Place on a jelly roll pan and bake at 350 degrees for 20 - 30 minutes or until done.

For sauce: In a deep frying pan, combine the sauce ingredients. Cook over low heat until smooth and melted. Add meatballs to pan and simmer for 30 - 45 minutes.

Makes 50 meatballs

Tip: Cranberries compliment venison. These meatballs are rich.

Venison Meatballs in Bourbon Sauce

Meatballs:

1-1/2 pounds ground venison
1/2 cup dry bread crumbs
1/2 cup milk
1 egg, beaten
1 garlic clove, finely minced
1/4 cup finely minced onion
1 teaspoon salt
1/4 teaspoon black pepper

Bourbon Sauce:

1 cup barbecue sauce (such as
   K.C. Masterpiece)
3/4 cup bourbon
1/4 cup honey
1/2 cup prepared mustard
   (spicy)
Dash of Worcestershire sauce

For meatballs: Mix ingredients well and shape into 1-inch balls. Place in a baking dish and brown in a 350-degree oven for 30 minutes. Drain well if needed.

For bourbon sauce: Cook sauce ingredients in a sauce pan over medium heat for 5 minutes. Add meatballs; bring to a boil. Reduce heat and simmer for 30 minutes. Serve hot as an appetizer.

Makes about 50 meatballs

Tip: These meatballs are also good in a quick and easy currant sauce. Heat a 10-ounce jar red currant jelly and a 12-ounce jar chili sauce (found near ketchup in the supermarket) in a large skillet. Add meatballs and simmer for 30 minutes. Serve hot in a chafing dish. This is a tried and true favorite recipe that frequently converts non-venison eaters. Currants really compliment venison.

Spanikopita

2 tablespoons olive oil
1/2 cup finely chopped onion
2 garlic cloves, minced
1/2 pound ground venison, crumbled
1/4 cup sun dried tomatoes
1 package (4 ounces) Crumbled Feta Cheese with Garlic and Herbs
1 package (4 ounces) Crumbled Feta Cheese with Basil and Tomato
2 packages (10 ounces each) frozen chopped spinach, defrosted and well drained
4 eggs, slightly beaten
1/3 cup sliced olives
1 tablespoon dried Greek Seasoning Blend (such as McCormick)
1/2 teaspoon Cavender's All-Purpose Greek Seasoning (see tips)
1/2 cup butter, melted
12 sheets phyllo (or fillo) dough (see tips)

Preheat oven to 350 degrees.

In a large skillet, heat 2 tablespoons olive oil. Sauté onion in oil until tender; add garlic and cook until garlic becomes fragrant. Add ground venison, stirring to crumble, and cook over medium heat for 3 - 5 minutes or until meat is no longer pink. During the last 2 minutes of cooking, add sun-dried tomatoes (which have been soaked in 1/4 cup hot water and then drained).

In a large mixing bowl, combine venison mixture, spinach, olives, feta cheeses, eggs and seasonings. Mix well.

Brush bottom and sides of a 9 x 13-inch baking dish with melted butter. Remove phyllo from package and cut to fit dish. Keep phyllo covered with damp paper towels to prevent it from drying out. Place 1 sheet phyllo in bottom of dish. Brush with melted butter. Continue layering and brushing with 5 more sheets. Spread spinach mixture evenly over phyllo. Layer and brush remaining 6 sheets as before. Cut spanikopita into 8 squares all the way through to the bottom. Be sure to cut before baking. Bake for 40 - 45 minutes or until golden brown.

Serves 6 - 8

Spanikopita *(cont.)*

Tips: Phyllo is a paper-thin dough that is most commonly available frozen. It should be kept covered (with damp paper towels or plastic wrap) and worked with quickly to keep it from drying out. This recipe does not use an entire package of phyllo dough.

To drain spinach well, place in a clean kitchen towel (not terry cloth) and twist to remove water. Spinach should become a dry ball.

Cavender's Greek Seasoning has a lot of salt; therefore, we use 2 Greek seasonings. There are numerous brands of dried Greek seasoning herb blends (such as McCormick). These do not have salt. The blends are handy because not as many different types of herbs are needed.

In some senses this dish might be termed a Greek-style quiche. Rest assured though, this is a hardy quiche for real men.

Southern-Style Shepherd's Pie

Pie:

2 tablespoons olive oil
1/2 cup chopped onion
1/2 cup chopped carrots
1/2 cup chopped celery
1/2 cup sliced mushrooms
1/2 pound ground venison
1 package (10 ounces) frozen
    baby lima beans
1 can (8.75 ounces) whole
    kernel corn
2 tablespoons tomato paste
1/4 teaspoon dried thyme
1/8 teaspoon ground red
    pepper (cayenne)
1 teaspoon Worcestershire
    sauce
1 teaspoon sweet paprika
1 tablespoon dried parsley
1 cup beef broth
1 tablespoon all-purpose flour
Salt to taste

Garlic Smashed Potatoes:

4 medium russet potatoes,
    peeled and chopped
3 whole garlic cloves, peeled
    and smashed
4 tablespoons butter
1/3 cup milk
2 tablespoons sour cream
Salt and freshly ground pepper
    to taste

1/4 cup freshly grated
    Parmesan cheese
1/2 cup grated cheddar cheese

Put potatoes and garlic in a large sauce pan and cover with cold water. Bring to a boil, add salt to taste and cook potatoes until tender (about 12 - 15 minutes).

Cook lima beans according to package directions.

While potatoes boil and limas cook, preheat a large skillet over medium-high heat. Add oil to pan and sauté onion, carrots, celery and mushrooms until tender (about 7 minutes). Stir in ground venison and cook until venison is no longer pink. Add cooked and drained lima beans and drained corn to mixture. Season with tomato paste, thyme, cayenne, Worcestershire, paprika and parsley. In a 1-cup measure, blend broth and flour until smooth. Stir broth mixture into venison and vegetables and heat to boiling. Boil until mixture thickens slightly. Taste and add salt if needed.

Place venison mixture in a sprayed 2 quart square casserole dish.

Drain potatoes; add butter, milk and sour cream and mash (with a potato masher) until potatoes are almost smooth. Salt and pepper potatoes to taste. Spread the mashed potatoes evenly over the meat mixture to form a crust. Sprinkle with cheeses. Bake in a 425-degree oven for 15 - 20 minutes or until potatoes are browned and casserole bubbles. Let stand 5 minutes before serving.

Serves 5 - 6

Southern-Style Shepherd's Pie *(cont.)*

Tips: If desired, canned limas can be used. Make sure the broth is absorbed by the meat-vegetables mixture so it does not bubble up through the potatoes. You may use leftover, cooked venison rather than raw. Be careful not to over mash the potatoes or they will become gluey. The potatoes are good as a side dish. Leftover potatoes can be used but the freshly smashed potatoes add a great deal to the pie.

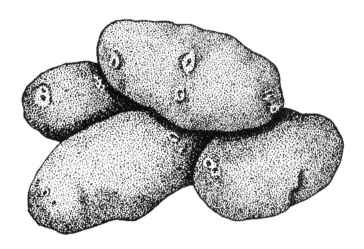

Stroganoff with Venison Meatballs

8 ounces wide egg noodles

Meatballs:

1 pound ground venison
12 saltine crackers, crushed
1/3 cup finely chopped onion
1 large egg, slightly beaten
1/4 teaspoon kosher salt
1 teaspoon dried parsley,
crushed
1/2 teaspoon freshly ground
black pepper
3 tablespoons water
2 tablespoons olive oil
2 tablespoons all-purpose flour
1 teaspoon sweet Hungarian
paprika
1/2 teaspoon kosher salt
1 can (14 ounces) chicken
broth
1/2 cup reduced-fat sour cream

In a medium bowl, combine ground venison, saltines, onion, egg, salt, parsley, black pepper and water. Shape into 1-inch meatballs, place on a cookie sheet and refrigerate for 30 minutes.

Cook egg noodles as directed on label.

Heat 2 tablespoons olive oil over medium-high heat until hot. Add meatballs and cook until meat is no longer pink (about 12 minutes), turning frequently to brown. Transfer meatballs to plate.

Stir flour into pan drippings and cook for 1 minute, stirring constantly. Add paprika and cook 30 seconds. Gradually stir in broth and bring to a boil; cook about 2 minutes or until slightly thickened. Add salt if needed. Reduce heat to low and stir in sour cream. Return meatballs to pan and heat through. Spoon meatball mixture over noodles to serve.

Serves 4 - 6

Tips: Refrigerating the meatballs makes them maintain their shape while cooking. Moisten your hands with water while shaping meatballs to prevent sticking. Kosher salt has a coarser texture than regular iodized salt. It can be found near other salts in the supermarket. 1-1/2 teaspoons iodized salt = 1 tablespoon kosher salt. Using kosher salt has helped us reduce our salt intake significantly.

Salisbury Steak with Mushroom Wine Gravy

3 tablespoons olive oil, divided
1 cup chopped onion, divided
1 garlic clove, minced
1 pound ground venison
1 egg, lightly beaten
1 slice bread, toasted and
 crumbled
1 teaspoon spicy brown
 mustard
1 teaspoon Worcestershire
 sauce
1 teaspoon Montreal Steak
 Seasoning, divided
1/2 teaspoon kosher salt
1 tablespoon dried parsley

1-1/2 cups sliced fresh
 mushrooms
1-1/2 tablespoons all-purpose
 flour
1/4 cup dry red wine
1 cup low-sodium beef broth
1/2 teaspoon freshly ground
 black pepper
Salt to taste, if needed

Sauté half of the chopped onion in 1 tablespoon hot olive oil in a medium skillet over medium-high heat until tender. Add garlic and sauté about 30 seconds. Remove from heat and cool slightly.

Combine venison, cooked onion and garlic, egg, crumbled toast, mustard, Worcestershire sauce, 1/2 teaspoon steak seasoning, salt and parsley. Gently shape into 4 patties. Cook patties in 1 tablespoon olive oil over medium-high heat for 3 - 4 minutes on each side or until browned (do not cook until done). Remove patties and place in a lightly sprayed (with Pam) baking dish.

Add remaining 1 tablespoon oil and half of chopped onion to drippings in skillet and sauté over medium heat until tender. Add mushrooms and sauté 3 minutes. Whisk in flour and cook, stirring constantly for 1 minute. Whisk in wine, broth, 1/2 teaspoon steak seasoning and additional salt (if needed). Bring to a boil; reduce heat to low and simmer, stirring occasionally, for about 5 minutes or until slightly thickened. Top patties with gravy. Bake, covered, at 350 degrees for 30 minutes or until done.

Serves 4

Quick Venison Mac

1/2 pound ground venison
1 tablespoon olive oil
1 small leek, cleaned and
   chopped (or onion)
1 garlic clove, minced
1 can (14 ounces) diced
   tomatoes
1 can (8 ounces) tomato sauce
1 cup water
1/4 teaspoon chili powder
1/8 teaspoon cumin
1/4 teaspoon sugar
1/4 teaspoon black pepper
1 cup uncooked elbow
   macaroni
3 tablespoons fresh oregano,
   chopped

In a skillet, brown venison, chopped leek and garlic in olive oil. Be sure to crumble venison as it cooks. Add tomatoes, tomato sauce and water and bring to a boil. Add all other ingredients except fresh oregano and return to a boil. Reduce heat, cover and simmer 15 minutes or until macaroni is tender. Add oregano and serve immediately.

Serves 3

Chopped Steak and Gravy

2 teaspoons dry beef onion
   soup mix
1/4 cup water
1 pound ground venison
1 teaspoon Worcestershire
   sauce
salt and pepper to taste
2 tablespoons olive oil
2 tablespoons flour
1 cup water

Microwave onion soup mix in 1/4 cup water until onions are tender and add to ground venison with Worcestershire sauce, salt and pepper. Handle gently and form into patties. Place olive oil in a non-stick skillet. Add patties and cook until done (6 - 8 minutes). Remove from the pan. Add 2 tablespoons flour and make a roux. Stir constantly for 1 minute. Add 1 – 1-1/2 cups water and stir until smooth and thick. Add patties and simmer 10 - 15 minutes. Serve with rice.

Serves 4

Venison Eggplant Parmigiana

1 large eggplant, or 3 - 4 small
   eggplants
Salt to taste
1 pound ground venison
1/2 cup chopped onion
2 garlic cloves, minced
1 tablespoon olive oil
1 can (16 ounces) diced
   tomatoes
1 can (8 ounces) tomato sauce
3 tablespoon fresh basil,
   chopped
1/2 teaspoon black pepper
1 tablespoon cherry preserves

1 egg, beaten
1/2 cup cracker crumbs
   (saltines)
1 - 2 tablespoons olive oil
2 cups shredded mozzarella
   cheese, divided

Peel and slice eggplant, place on paper towels and sprinkle with salt; cover with more paper towels. Let set while preparing sauce.

In a large skillet, sauté venison, onion and garlic in 1 tablespoon olive oil until meat is no longer pink. Add tomatoes, tomato sauce, basil, salt and pepper and cherry preserves. Stir well and simmer for 15 - 20 minutes.

Rinse eggplant and pat dry. Dip in egg and then cracker crumbs and quickly brown in 1 - 2 tablespoons of the olive oil. Spray a baking dish. Layer eggplant, 1 cup of cheese, sauce and remainder of cheese. Bake uncovered at 350 degrees for 15 - 20 minutes until bubbly and hot.

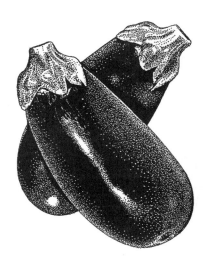

Deep Dish Potato and Venison Pie

**Pastry for double-crust pie
  (homemade or purchased)**
1 cup grated, peeled potatoes
1/4 cup chopped celery
1/2 cup grated carrots
1/4 cup chopped leeks
**2 teaspoons Worcestershire
  sauce**
1 teaspoon A-1 Steak Sauce
**1 teaspoon dried Italian
  seasoning**
**1/4 teaspoon freshly ground
  black pepper**
Salt to taste
**1 pound uncooked ground
  venison**

Place bottom crust in 9-inch deep-dish pie plate. Mix all other ingredients and place in pie crust. Place top crust on pie and seal edges. Cut vents in top pastry. Bake at 375 for 15 minutes. Reduce heat to 350 degrees and bake for 55 minutes to 1 hour. This pie is hearty; however, it is dry and needs to be served with a sauce. We like this mushroom sauce.

Mushroom Sauce:

**2 tablespoons margarine or
  butter**
1/4 cup sliced leeks
**2 cups sliced fresh mushrooms
  (wild or button)**
2 tablespoons flour
1 cup half-and-half
Salt and pepper to taste

Melt margarine and sauté leeks and mushrooms until tender. Sprinkle with flour and cook about 1 minute. Add half-and-half and seasonings. Continue cooking until sauce has thickened. Stir constantly. Serve over pie slices.

Tip: This sauce can also be used over steaks, chops or wild rice with upland game.

Bacon Mushroom Swiss Meat Loaf

4 slices diced bacon
1 cup chopped mushrooms
1/4 cup finely chopped onion
1 pound ground venison
1 egg
1/4 cup milk
1 cup shredded Swiss cheese
1/2 cup very fine corn flake
  crumbs
1/4 teaspoon salt
1/8 teaspoon black pepper

In a large skillet, cook bacon until crisp. Remove bacon with a slotted spoon to paper towels to drain. Remove all but one tablespoon of bacon drippings; sauté the mushrooms and onions in drippings until tender. Allow to cool slightly. In a large bowl, mix the venison, egg and milk. Add the mushroom/onion mixture, Swiss cheese (except for a few tablespoons), the bacon crumbs (except for a tablespoon) and corn flake crumbs; mix well until blended. Place in a large loaf pan and bake at 350 degrees for 1 hour or until cooked through. If your ground venison is not lean, drain the fat. Sprinkle top of meatloaf with reserved cheese and bacon. Bake an additional 5 minutes or until cheese melts. Let meatloaf rest for 10 minutes before slicing.

Serves 4 - 6

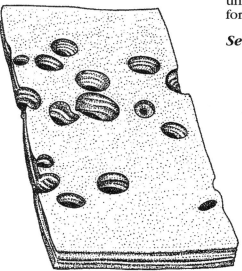

E.T.'s Meat Loaf

1-1/2 to 2 pounds ground
   venison
1 package dry onion soup mix
1 cup oats, regular or quick
   cooking (not instant)
1 egg, slightly beaten
1/2 cup applesauce
1/2 cup ketchup, divided
Black pepper to taste

Thoroughly mix all ingredients using only 1/4 cup ketchup. Place in loaf pan and bake at 350 degrees for 45 - 50 minutes. Remove from oven and top with remaining 1/4 cup ketchup. Return to oven for 10 - 15 minutes or until top is browned and meat loaf is done.

Tip: The applesauce really makes this meat loaf moist and tasty.

Cranberry Topped Meat Loaf

1/4 cup cranberry sauce
1/8 - 1/4 cup brown sugar
1 pound ground venison
1/2 cup quick cooking oats
1/2 cup milk
1/4 cup finely chopped onion
1/8 cup ketchup
1/8 cup cocktail sauce
1 egg, slightly beaten
1/2 teaspoon Italian seasoning
1/8 teaspoon black pepper
1/2 teaspoon salt or to taste

Preheat oven to 350 degrees. Spray a 9 x 5 x 3-inch loaf pan. In a small bowl, combine the cranberry sauce and brown sugar. Place sauce mixture in bottom of a loaf pan. In a large bowl, combine the remaining ingredients and mix well. Place in loaf pan on top of cranberry sauce mixture. Bake at 350 for 1 hour. Allow loaf to cool for about 10 minutes before carefully turning onto a serving plate so that the sauce side is up. Serve immediately.

Banana Meat Loaf

1 pound ground venison
1/2 cup soft bread crumbs
1/2 cup oats
1/2 teaspoon Hungarian sweet
   paprika
1/2 teaspoon salt
1/4 teaspoon black pepper
1 tablespoon finely diced onion
3/4 cup mashed firm bananas
1/2 teaspoon dry mustard

Combine all ingredients well. Place in a loaf pan (spray pan with Pam) and bake at 350 for 45 minutes to 1 hour or until done.

Serves 3 - 4

Tip: This meat loaf is an off-beat, interesting and tasty combination.

Simple Venison Meat Loaf

1-1/2 pounds ground venison
1 egg, slightly beaten
1/3 cup ketchup
1 tablespoons onion, finely
   diced
1 cup quick cooking oats
3/4 cup milk
1 teaspoon kosher salt
1/2 teaspoon black pepper

Mix well but gently and place in a loaf pan. Using a spoon, make an indentation down the center of the meat loaf. Fill with additional ketchup. Bake at 350 degrees for 1 hour. Serve with ketchup or tomato gravy.

Serves 6

Tip: Add mashed potatoes and green beans for a comforting meal.

Sloppy Joe's on Corn Bread

1 tablespoon olive oil
1/2 pound ground venison
1/4 cup chopped onion
1/4 cup chopped bell pepper,
   optional
1/2 cup chopped celery
1 large carrot, grated
1 can (8 ounces) tomato sauce
1/4 cup ketchup
1/4 teaspoon black pepper
1/2 teaspoon salt
1-1/2 teaspoons Worcestershire
   sauce

Brown ground venison and onion in olive oil in a skillet. Add all other ingredients and simmer for 15 - 20 minutes until vegetables are tender and sauce has thickened. Serve over hot corn bread. Hamburger buns may be used if preferred.

Serves 2

Garlic Venison

4 tablespoons olive oil, divided
4 - 6 cloves garlic
1 pound ground venison
1/2 teaspoon salt
Ground black pepper (or red pepper) to taste
1 package (8 ounces) macaroni pasta

Cook macaroni according to package directions, but add 2 tablespoons olive oil to water as pasta cooks.

Place remaining two tablespoons olive oil in a heated skillet; add garlic and cook briefly (until fragrant). Add ground venison and cook until browned. Season with salt and pepper.

Serve garlic-flavored meat over macaroni.

Serves 3 - 4

Taco Corn Bread Pizza

1 package (8.5 ounces) corn
 bread mix
2 tablespoons olive oil, divided
1 pound ground venison
1 package (1.25 ounces) taco
 seasoning mix
1 to 1-1/2 cups white cheddar
 cheese
1/2 cup sliced black olives

For garnish: fresh cilantro,
 salsa, guacamole and sour
 cream

Preheat oven to 400 degrees.
Spread 1 tablespoon oil on a 12-inch pizza pan, being sure pan is
well coated.

Prepare corn bread mix by
package directions and spread
batter onto prepared pizza pan.
Bake 8 - 10 minutes or until lightly
browned.

Meanwhile, heat remaining olive
oil in skillet and brown venison
until no longer pink. Add taco-seasoning mix and prepare
according to package directions.
Simmer to reduce liquid.

When corn bread crust is
removed from the oven, sprinkle it
with 1/2 cup cheese. Add venison
mixture, top with sliced olives and
remaining cheese. Bake 4 - 5
minutes or until cheese is melted.
Top with desired garnishes.

Serves 4 - 6

*Tips: Try using a paper towel to spread oil evenly onto the pizza pan. If
you don't like spicy foods, use only half of the taco seasoning mix.
Lawry's makes a taco seasoning that is particularly tasty with venison.*

Meal in a Skillet

2 tablespoons olive oil
1/4 cup chopped onion
1/2 pound ground venison
1 can (10 ounces) diced
   tomatoes with green chiles
3/4 cup water
1/2 cup uncooked long-grain
   rice
1/2 envelope (1.25 ounces) taco
   seasoning
1/2 teaspoon cilantro
Salt to taste
1 cup shredded Mexican cheese
   blend
2 cups shredded lettuce
1 tomato, chopped
1 avocado, sliced
1 can (2.25 ounces) sliced black
   olives
3 - 4 tablespoons sour cream
Salsa
Tortilla chips

Heat olive oil in a large skillet over medium-high heat. Sauté onion until tender. Add ground venison and cook until venison is no longer pink. Stir in tomatoes, water, rice, taco seasoning and cilantro. Cook, covered, over medium heat 15 minutes, stirring occasionally. Uncover and cook until rice is tender (5 - 10 more minutes). Up to 1/2 cup additional water can be added if rice is not done; however, cook until water has cooked out and rice and meat are thick. Remove from heat. Top with cheese, lettuce, tomato, avocado, black olives, sour cream and salsa. Stand tortilla chips around edge of skillet and serve immediately with additional chips.

Serves 3 - 4

Enchilada Casserole

1 tablespoon olive oil
1/2 cup chopped onion
1 garlic clove, minced
1 pound ground venison
1 can (16 ounces) pinto beans, rinsed and drained
1 can (10.75 ounces) cream of mushroom soup
1 teaspoon cumin
1/2 teaspoon dried cilantro
1/2 teaspoon dried oregano
1/2 teaspoon dried ancho chile pepper
1/2 cup reduced-fat sour cream
1 can (14 ounces) enchilada sauce, divided
12 corn (6 inch) tortillas
2 cups Mexican blend shredded cheese

Preheat oven to 350 degrees. Coat an 8 x 11-inch baking dish with cooking spray. Spread half of the enchilada sauce over the bottom of the baking dish; set aside.

In a large skillet, heat 1 tablespoon olive oil and sauté onion until tender. Add garlic and sauté about 1 minute. Add ground venison and cook until venison is browned completely. Drain if necessary.

Add beans, soup, cumin, cilantro, oregano and ancho chile pepper to meat; continue cooking until bubbly. Stir in sour cream and heat thoroughly.

Place 4 tortillas in baking dish on top of enchilada sauce, tearing to cover. Top with half the meat mixture and 1/3 of cheese. Repeat once more with 4 more tortillas, remaining meat and 1/3 cheese. Top with remaining 4 tortillas and remaining enchilada sauce. Cover tightly with foil that has been coated with cooking spray (or use the release foil).

Bake 45 minutes. Remove cover. Sprinkle with remaining cheese and bake, uncovered, 10 - 15 minutes or until cheese is melted. Serve immediately. Garnish with sour cream and salsa.

Serves 6

Mexican Casserole

1 tablespoon olive oil
1/2 cup chopped onion
1 garlic clove, minced
1 pound ground venison
1 can (8 ounces) tomato sauce
1 can (14 ounces) diced
   tomatoes, undrained
1 can (16 ounces) pinto beans,
   rinsed and drained
1 can (4.5 ounces) chopped
   green chiles, undrained (see
   tips)
2 teaspoons chili powder
1/2 teaspoon ground ancho
   chile pepper
1 teaspoon ground cumin
1/2 teaspoon dried oregano
Salt to taste

Corn Bread Mix:

1 package (8.5 ounces) corn
   bread mix (see tips)
1 egg
1 cup buttermilk
1 can (8.75 ounces) whole
   kernel corn, drained

Heat olive oil in a deep skillet. Sauté onion until tender; add garlic and sauté briefly. Add ground venison and cook until browned; stir to crumble meat. Add tomato sauce, tomatoes, beans, chiles and all seasonings. Bring to a boil and reduce heat. Simmer (uncovered) until slightly thickened (20 - 30 minutes). Pour meat/bean mixture into an 11 x 7-inch casserole dish.

Prepare corn bread mix by using 1 egg and 1 cup buttermilk. Mix well and stir in drained corn. Pour over casserole and spread evenly.

Bake at 350 degrees for 30 - 35 minutes or until casserole is bubbling and corn bread is golden.

Serves 4 - 6

Tips: If you do not like hot and spicy foods, decrease the chopped green chiles. One tablespoon is enough for a milder dish. The corn muffin mix is too sweet for this dish.

Tortilla Stack

1 can (9 ounces) bean dip
2 tablespoons plus 1/4 cup sour cream
1 teaspoon plus 1/4 teaspoon cumin
2 cups cooked ground venison
1/2 cup thinly sliced green onions with tops
3/4 cup sliced pitted ripe olives, divided
1/4 cup snipped fresh cilantro, divided
5 flour tortilla, 10-inch size
2 cups cheddar cheese, shredded
Vegetable oil
2 medium plum tomatoes, seeded and chopped
Salsa for garnish if desired

Preheat oven to 375 degrees. Combine bean dip, 2 tablespoons sour cream and 1 teaspoon cumin in a bowl; mix well.

Cook ground venison until browned and crumble. Add green onions, 1/2 cup of the olives and 2 tablespoons of fresh cilantro to ground venison.

Place 1 tortilla on a baking stone or pizza pan. Top tortilla with several tablespoons of bean mixture; spread to within 1/4-inch of edge of tortilla. Top evenly with venison mixture and 1/2 cup shredded cheese. Repeat layers of tortilla, bean mixture, venison mixture and cheese 3 more times. Top with remaining tortilla and brush with vegetable oil.

Bake 25-30 minutes or until top is golden brown. Mix the remaining 1/4 cup sour cream with 1/4 teaspoon cumin and spread evenly over top of warm tortilla stack. Sprinkle with tomato, remaining 1/4 cup olive slices and cilantro. Cut into wedges and serve with salsa if desired.

Serves 6

Taco Cheesecake

1-1/4 cups crushed tortilla chips
1 tablespoon butter, melted
1 pound ground venison
1 envelope (1.25 ounces) taco seasoning mix, divided
2 tablespoons water
2 packages (8 ounces each) reduced-fat cream cheese
2 eggs
2 cups shredded Mexican cheese blend
1 container (8 ounces) sour cream
2 tablespoons flour
Optional toppings: shredded lettuce, chopped tomato, chopped bell pepper, chopped avocado, sliced olives

Combine crushed tortilla chips and butter. Press into bottom of a 9-inch spring form pan. Bake at 325 degrees for 10 minutes. Cool on a wire rack.

Cook venison in a large skillet over medium heat until it crumbles and is no longer pink. Drain, if necessary, and pat dry with paper towels. Return venison to skillet. Reserve 1 teaspoon taco seasoning mix. Stir remaining taco seasoning mix and 2 tablespoons water into venison. Cook over medium heat until liquid evaporates (about 5 minutes).

Beat cream cheese at medium speed with an electric mixer until fluffy; add eggs, reserved taco seasoning mix and Mexican cheese; beat until blended.

Spread cream cheese mix evenly over crust and 1 inch up the sides of pan making an opening in the center. Spoon the venison mixture into the center. Combine sour cream and flour; spread over cheesecake.

Bake at 325 degrees for 25-30 minutes. Cool in pan on a wire rack for 10 minutes. Run a knife around the edges; release sides of pan. Serve warm with toppings, if desired.

Serves 6 - 8 (or 12 - 16 appetizer servings)

Tips: This savory cheesecake is great to use as an appetizer. If you prepare the cheesecake in advance and refrigerate, it takes a little longer to heat.

Mexican Lasagna

1 tablespoon vegetable oil
1 pound ground venison
1/2 medium onion, chopped
1 - 2 tablespoons chili powder
1/2 teaspoon cumin
10 tortillas, divided
1 can pinto beans, rinsed and
   drained
1 - 2 teaspoons canned green
   chiles
1 pound shredded Mexican
   cheese blend
1 can (10.75 ounces) cream of
   mushroom soup
1 can (14.5 ounces) diced (or
   Rotel) tomatoes, undrained

Brown ground venison and onion in oil; drain excess grease if needed. Add chili powder and cumin to meat and cook a minute or two to release flavors. Line an 11 x 14-inch pan with 5 tortillas cut into strips. Pour meat over them, add beans, desired amount of chiles and cheese. Place rest of tortillas cut into strips on top. Place dollops of mushroom soup over tortillas and top with tomatoes. Bake at 350 degrees for 40 minutes.

Serves 6

Enchiladas

12 tortillas

Enchilada Filling:

**1 to 1-1/2 pounds ground
venison**

1 medium onion, diced

3 cups Monterey Jack cheese

Enchilada Sauce:

**1 can (10.75 ounces) cream of
chicken soup**

**1 can (10 ounces) diced
tomatoes and chilies**

1/2 cup onion, diced

**1 can (4 ounces) chopped
green chilies**

Wrap tortillas in foil and place in a moderate oven to soften (8 - 10 minutes).

Meanwhile, sauté ground venison and onion in a skillet until venison is no longer pink and onion is tender. Place a little meat and onion mixture on a softened tortilla, add a little cheese, roll up tortilla and place in a lightly greased baking dish. Repeat with other tortillas.

Mix all sauce ingredients together and pour over rolled tortillas. Pour any remaining meat over sauce. Top with remaining cheese. Bake in a 350-degree oven until hot and bubbly (about 20 - 30 minutes).

Serves 6

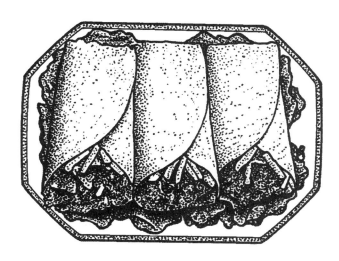

Special Blue Burgers

1 pound ground venison
1 teaspoon Montreal Steak
   Seasoning, or your favorite
   seasoning
4 tablespoons blue cheese
   crumbles, divided
1-1/2 teaspoons olive oil
1-1/2 teaspoons
   Worcestershire sauce

Gently mix ground venison and steak seasoning and form into four burgers. Make an indentation in the center of each burger and add 1 tablespoon blue cheese crumbles to each burger. Carefully wrap meat around cheese being sure to totally enclose cheese. Place burgers on platter and drizzle olive oil and Worcestershire sauce over burgers, turning to coat well. Let burgers come to room temperature while grill preheats. Grill 6 - 7 minutes per side over medium heat. Serve on toasted buns with condiments of your choice, such as lettuce, tomato, pickles and onions.

Serves 4

Tip: Montreal Steak Seasoning is available in the spice and herb section of most grocery stores. McCormick is a brand that is widely available.

Cook Out Time Burgers

2 pounds ground venison

Handle ground venison gently and form into 8 patties. Grill until desired doneness is reached (about 4 - 5 minutes per side) and serve with a variety of buns and Mustard Sauce, Herb Mayonnaise, Bacon Bean Topping, Vidalia Onion Marmalade and Double Red Topping.

Sit back and listen to the raves.

Serves 6 - 8

Mustard Sauce:

1/2 cup mayonnaise
3/4 cup sour cream
1 teaspoon dry mustard
2 teaspoons spicy brown mustard

Using a wire whisk mix above ingredients well. Serve as a condiment for venison burgers.

Herb Mayonnaise:

3 tablespoons mayonnaise
1 teaspoon Dijon mustard
1 teaspoon dried basil leaves
1/4 teaspoon dried parsley
1/2 teaspoon garlic salt
1/4 teaspoon freshly ground black pepper

Mix above ingredients well using a wire whisk. Serve as a venison burger condiment.

Bacon Bean Topping:

4 slices bacon
1/4 – 1/2 cup chopped onion
1 can (16 ounces) baked beans
2 tablespoons mustard

Pan fry bacon slices until crisp. Drain on paper towels and then crumble. Add onion to bacon drippings and sauté until tender. Add beans and mustard to onions and heat thoroughly. Place in a bowl and top with crumbled bacon. Serve over venison burgers or hot dogs.

Vidalia Onion Marmalade:

2 tablespoons olive oil
1 tablespoon butter
2 large Vidalia onions, thinly sliced and separated into rings
3/4 cup zinfandel wine
1 teaspoon dried basil, crushed
1/2 teaspoon salt
1/2 teaspoon black pepper

Heat oil and butter in a large skillet over medium-high heat. Add onions and cook for 5 - 7 minutes or until tender crisp. Add wine, basil, salt and pepper. Cook until most of the liquid has evaporated. Serve over venison burgers or steaks.

Cook Out Time Burgers *(cont.)*

Double Red Topper for Burgers:

2 tomatoes, sliced
1 medium red onion, sliced

Dressing:

2 tablespoons olive oil
2 teaspoons lemon juice
1 tablespoon fresh basil, chopped *or* 1 teaspoon dried basil
Salt and pepper to taste

Slice onion and soak in iced water for 10 - 15 minutes. Drain well. Mix dressing ingredients with a wire whisk. Pour over sliced tomatoes and red onions and toss. Serve on burgers or as a side dish.

Tips: Soaking the onion in iced water helps remove some of the sharpness. Yellow and red tomatoes offer an interesting color contrast.

Mexican Burgers

1 pound ground venison
1/4 cup finely chopped onion
1/2 - 1 teaspoon chili powder (or to taste)
1/4 teaspoon ground cumin
1/2 teaspoon finely minced jalapeno pepper (or to taste)
1/2 teaspoon salt
1/4 teaspoon black pepper

Combine all ingredients well and shape into 4 patties. Grill, broil or pan fry to desired doneness. Serve burgers on tortillas (cut burgers in half for a better fit), pita bread, English muffins or hamburger buns with traditional taco toppings of your choice.

Tips: The toppings might include salsa, shredded cheese, guacamole or chopped avocado, sour cream, lettuce, tomato and diced green onions. Serve with Corona and lime wedges or Mexican beer.

Italian Burgers

1 egg
1/4 cup oats, regular or quick
   cooking (do not use instant)
2 tablespoons ketchup
3/4 teaspoon dried Italian
   seasoning
1 garlic clove, finely minced
2 tablespoons finely chopped
   onion
1/4 teaspoon salt
1 pound ground venison

4 mozzarella cheese slices
4 hamburger buns or rolls

Lightly beat egg with a fork and stir in oats. Add ketchup, Italian seasoning, garlic, onion, salt and ground venison. Mix well and shape into 4 patties. Broil or grill patties about 12 minutes or until desired doneness is reached, turning once. Top with cheese and broil until cheese melts. Serve on toasted buns with ketchup, lettuce and tomatoes.

Serves 4

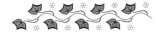

Feta Burgers

1/4 cup feta cheese
1 cup plain yogurt
1/4 – 1/2 teaspoon ground
   cumin

1 pound ground venison
1/4 cup finely diced onion
1/2 teaspoon dried cilantro, or
   to taste
Several dashes of ground
   ginger, or to taste
Salt to taste

Lettuce
Cucumbers, sliced thinly
Pita Bread

Blend feta cheese, yogurt and cumin with a fork until the cheese is finely crumbled. Cover and refrigerate for 1 hour.
   Combine ground venison, onion, cilantro, ginger and salt to taste. Shape into 4 patties and grill, broil or pan fry until done.
   Place lettuce and cucumbers in pita bread, add burger and top with 2 tablespoons feta cheese yogurt.

Serves 4

Burgers with Blue Cheese

1 pound ground venison
1/4 cup finely chopped onion
1/4 cup crumbled blue cheese
1 teaspoon Worcestershire
   sauce
1/4 teaspoon salt
1/8 teaspoon freshly ground
   black pepper

Mix all ingredients thoroughly but gently and shape into 4 patties. Grill over hot coals (about 4 minutes per side) or until burgers have reached desired doneness. Serve on grilled hamburger buns with lots of crisp lettuce, tomato slices and mayonnaise.

Serves 4

Tip: These can be broiled or cooked in a grilling pan; if grilling, oil the grill top to prevent sticking.

Burgers with Built-In Condiments

1 pound ground venison
2 tablespoons ketchup
1 tablespoon A-1 Steak Sauce
2 teaspoons mustard
1/2 teaspoon Worcestershire
   sauce
Several dashes freshly ground
   black pepper

Thoroughly mix all condiments into ground venison. Form into patties being careful to form well because condiments make burgers softer. Grill to desired doneness and serve on onion rolls with lettuce, tomato, onion and pickles.

Serves 4

Mustard Burgers

1 teaspoon Worcestershire
  sauce
1 pound ground venison
Mustard (such as Spicy Brown
  Mustard)

Mix Worcestershire sauce into ground venison and form into patties. Brush mustard onto both sides of patties and grill (using a grilling pan). Do not have heat too high or mustard will burn. Turn frequently and continue to lightly coat with mustard. Burgers are best if still slightly pink on the inside. Serve with lettuce, tomatoes, pickles and mustard on whole-wheat buns.

Serves 4

Chili Sauce for Burgers or Hot Dogs

2 tablespoons canola oil
1/2 cup finely chopped onion
2 garlic cloves, minced
1 pound ground venison, finely
  ground
1/2 teaspoon salt
1/2 teaspoon freshly ground
  black pepper
1 tablespoon yellow mustard
1 tablespoon cider vinegar
1 teaspoon Worcestershire
  sauce
Several dashes hot sauce, or to
  taste
1/4 cup ketchup
1 cup tomato juice

Heat oil to medium heat in a large heavy skillet and sauté onion and garlic until tender. Do not brown. Add venison and cook until meat is browned; stir frequently to break up any chunks of meat. Add remaining ingredients, bring to a boil, reduce heat and simmer until sauce has thickened. You may need to add more or less tomato juice to maintain the correct consistency. Serve over venison burgers with mustard, slaw and onions for a delicious treat or as a topping for hot dogs.

Serves 6 - 8

Tip: The secret to chili sauce is a uniform, non-chunky consistency. Try grinding the venison yourself in your food processor or blender. It needs to be very fine. The ideal chili sauce should not be lumpy.

Flavorful Burgers

1 pound ground venison

1/2 cup tomato and basil pasta sauce

1/3 cup finely chopped onion

1 garlic clove, finely minced

1 tablespoon dried parsley flakes

1/2 teaspoon onion salt

1/4 cup Italian-seasoned bread crumbs

1/4 cup freshly grated Parmesan cheese

4 mozzarella slices

4 onion rolls or buns (rub with a garlic clove)

Mix ingredients well and form into four patties. Place on preheated and prepared grill and cook until done. Top with cheese slices and cover grill to melt cheese. Rub rolls with garlic clove and toast on grill. Serve burgers with lettuce and tomato or additional pasta sauce.

Serves 4

Tip: Ground turkey can replace the venison.

Twelve Scrumptious Burger Sauces

1. Peachy Ketchup

1 cup ketchup
1/2 cup thick-and-spicy
    barbecue sauce
1/2 cup peach preserves

Stir all ingredients together until blended. Cover and chill for 2 hours.

2. Spicy Honey Ketchup

1 cup ketchup
2 tablespoons to 1/4 cup honey
1 tablespoon lime juice
1 teaspoon dried chipotle chile
    pepper

Stir all ingredients together until blended. Cover and chill 2 hours.

3. "Secret" Sauce

1 cup mayonnaise
1/3 cup ketchup
3 tablespoons sweet pickle
    relish

Stir all ingredients together until blended. Cover and chill 2 hours.

Tip: Try this on fish sandwiches.

4. Horseradish Spread

1 package (8 ounces) cream
    cheese, softened
2 tablespoons Dijon mustard
2 tablespoons prepared
    horseradish

Stir all ingredients together until well blended. Cover and chill 1 hour.

5. Caper Mayo

1 cup mayonnaise
1 tablespoon undrained capers

Stir to blend well. Serve immediately.

6. Cucumber-Yogurt Sauce

1 cup (8 ounces) plain low fat
    yogurt
1 cup finely diced, seeded
    cucumber
1/2 teaspoon finely minced
    garlic
1/2 teaspoon dried dill weed

Stir all ingredients together, cover and refrigerate.

Tip: To remove cucumber seeds, cut the cucumber in half lengthwise and scrape a teaspoon down the middle.

7. Horseradish Mustard

1/2 cup Dijon mustard
1 tablespoon finely grated
   fresh horseradish, *or*
   prepared horseradish,
   drained

Mix the mustard and horseradish together. Serve at room temperature. May be refrigerated up to 1 week.

8. Basil Mayo

2 cups mayonnaise
1 cup fresh basil leaves
Salt and pepper to taste

Place all ingredients in a blender and puree until smooth.

9. Balsamic Mayo

3 tablespoons aged Balsamic
   vinegar
1/2 cup mayonnaise (or
   reduced-fat mayonnaise)
Coarse black pepper to taste

Stir all ingredients to mix well. Refrigerate. Serve with burgers.

10. Dried Tomato Sauce

1/3 cup minced dried tomatoes
   packed in oil, drained
1/3 cup plain nonfat yogurt
1-1/2 teaspoons dried basil

Stir together all ingredients until well blended; chill, if desired.

11. Southwestern Sauce

3/4 cup buttermilk Ranch
   dressing
1/2 cup chunky salsa

Stir ingredients together and serve with burgers.

Tip: For a nice salad, toss sauce with torn romaine lettuce and sprinkle with crushed tortilla chips.

12. Lemon, Garlic and Parsley Butter

4 tablespoons unsalted butter,
   softened
1/2 teaspoon grated lemon zest
1 garlic clove, finely minced
1 tablespoon minced fresh
   parsley
1/2 teaspoon salt
1/4 teaspoon freshly ground
   black pepper

Using a fork, mix ingredients until combined. Just before serving, spoon about 1 tablespoon butter onto each burger.

Tip: Other compound butters can be used also. Compound butters compliment venison steaks a great deal.

A Dozen Ways to Jazz Up a Burger

1. Add 1/4 cup Karo Light Corn Syrup to 1 pound ground venison for extra-moist burgers. Your favorite herbs or spices can be added also.

Tip: This will be a pleasant surprise – the burgers are moist and there is no sweet taste.

2. Add 1 tablespoon steak sauce to 1 pound ground venison and shape into patties.

3. Make venison burger patties and place on a platter. Drizzle patties with Worcestershire sauce (1 tablespoon per 2 pounds venison) and olive oil (1 tablespoon per 2 pounds venison). Let patties come to room temperature before grilling.

4. Serve burgers open-face style and top with salsa.

Fresh Tomato-Herb Salsa

4 large, fresh, plum tomatoes
1/4 cup chopped fresh basil
1 shallot, minced
2 tablespoons balsamic vinegar
1 tablespoon olive oil
Salt and black pepper to taste
     Peel tomatoes. Cut in half; squeeze out juices. Chop tomatoes; add basil, shallot, vinegar and oil. Season with salt and pepper. Serve on burgers.

Tip: This salsa is excellent on fish.

A Dozen Ways to Jazz Up a Burger *(cont.)*

5. Here is another salsa that compliments venison burgers.

Corn, Black Bean and Tomato Salsa

2 cups seeded, diced fresh tomatoes
1 can (16 ounces) black beans, drained and rinsed
3 ears fresh corn, cooked, cooled and cut off cob
1 green onion, thinly sliced
1 tablespoon minced fresh cilantro leaves
2 tablespoons freshly squeezed lime juice
1 tablespoon dried parsley
1 garlic clove, minced
2 tablespoons extra virgin olive oil
1 teaspoon minced canned chipotle pepper in adobo sauce
1/4 teaspoon adobo sauce from peppers
1/4 teaspoon salt
   Combine all ingredients in a medium bowl and stir to blend. Cover and refrigerate before serving.

Tip: This salsa is also delicious with beef, pork or fish.

6. Balsamic vinegar intensifies the flavor of tomatoes. The flavors enhance a venison burger tremendously.

Balsamic-Marinated Tomatoes

4 large tomatoes, cut into 1/2-inch-thick slices
1-1/2 tablespoons balsamic vinegar
1/4 cup chopped fresh basil
Salt and black pepper to taste
   Arrange tomato slices in a single layer in a 9 x 13-inch glass dish. Sprinkle sliced tomatoes with salt and pepper, then balsamic vinegar and chopped fresh basil. Let stand at least 1 hour and up to 3 hours, turning tomato slices once. Serve as topper for venison burgers.

A Dozen Ways to Jazz Up a Burger *(cont.)*

7. _Grilled Vidalia Onions_

1 Vidalia onion, sliced crosswise 1/2-inch thick (do not separate into rings)
Olive oil for brushing
Salt and black pepper

Brush onion slices with olive oil on both sides and season with salt and pepper. Grill until golden brown (3 - 4 minutes per side). Serve on venison burgers.

Tip: Placing wooden skewers through the slices prevents the onion from separating into rings while cooking.

8. Try guacamole burgers for a change.

Guacamole

1 avocado (preferably Haas)
2-1/2 teaspoons fresh lime juice (or lemon juice)
1/3 cup finely diced seeded tomato
3 tablespoons minced green onion
1/4 teaspoon ground cumin
2 tablespoons chopped fresh cilantro (or to taste)

Halve, pit and peel the avocado. Mash the avocado flesh with a fork, and stir in remaining ingredients. Place venison burgers on buns and top with guacamole.

9. Different breads can make a basic burger special. Some options are: Italian bread, French bread, rye bread, sourdough roll, soft roll, sour dough English muffin, flour or corn tortilla, focaccia bread, pita bread, sesame-seed roll, whole-wheat or multi-grain bread and pumpernickel bread.

10. A smear of pesto and a thick slice of home-grown tomato makes a venison burger a summertime delight.

11. Instead of lettuce, try sprouts, fresh herbs, coleslaw or spinach.

12. Flavored mustards, chutneys and barbecue sauces take burgers beyond the ordinary.

General Burger Tips

1. Be careful not to overmix ground meats – doing so will make the patties dense.

2. Use a light hand when shaping the burgers so they don't become too compacted.

3. To keep meat from sticking to you as you form the patties, work with damp hands.

4. Resist the urge to press the burgers with a spatula as they cook – you will press away flavorful juices.

5. Avoid frequent turning of patties to keep burgers from crumbling.

6. Freeze uncooked burgers in a heavy-duty plastic bag for up to 3 months; place the burgers between sheets of wax paper or plastic wrap to make separation of frozen burgers easier.

Chapter 5

Hearty Offerings for the Hungry: Soups and Stews

In cold or inclement weather, when hearth and home seem the best of all places to be, nothing stokes and satisfies the inner man better than a hearty soup or a savory stew. Venison lends itself to such dishes in exceptionally fine fashion. Whether it involves ground meat in a soup or chunks of venison in a stew, the end result is something to soothe the hungry soul and tame the turbulent beast.

With the addition of herbs and spices, along with some ingenuity and a bit of inventiveness, it is possible to produce dishes of this sort that offer delightful dining diversity. When accompanied by a sandwich, or maybe some crackers or a piece of cornbread, soup makes a simple, satisfying way to enjoy lunch or dinner. For those watching their weight, substituting a salad or some fruit for these accompaniments to soup will keep the calories under control. Also, soup is a dish that keeps well and can be ready to eat after just a few moments in a microwave. We often make a big pot, eat some of it at the time, and then freeze the rest for future use.

Stew, on the other hand, depending on its nature, can be a main dish or stand alone. In the case of stews where chunks of venison sidle up to an impressive array of vegetables, you may want nothing more than a piece of bread or a fruit salad to make a memorable, satisfying meal.

Best of all, the way soups and stews are prepared means that inferior cuts suddenly become superior dishes. All it takes is the simple magic of time and the right blend of ingredients to make this transition. Hold this chapter and its recipes close to the heart in the grim, grey days of winter. You'll find that sampling this fare will brighten your days and lighten your ways.

Pasta e Fagoli

1/2 cup chopped onion
2 garlic cloves, minced
1/2 cup chopped celery
1/2 cup grated carrots
2 tablespoons olive oil
1 can (14 ounces) chicken
  broth
1/2 pound ground venison,
  browned
2 cans (14 ounces each) diced
  tomatoes
1 can (8 ounces) tomato sauce
1 can (16 ounces) red kidney
  beans
1 can (19 ounces) white kidney
  beans (cannellini)
1 cup chopped, cooked ziti *or*
  ditalini
1/2 teaspoon black pepper
1 teaspoon dried parsley
1/2 teaspoon dried basil
1-1/2 teaspoons Italian
  seasonings
Salt to taste

Sauté onion, garlic, celery and carrots in olive oil until tender crisp. Add chicken broth and simmer. Brown ground venison. Add venison, diced tomatoes and tomato sauce to vegetable mixture. Drain and rinse red and white kidney beans; add to soup. Cook ziti (or other small pasta) and chop with scissors; add to soup. Add seasonings. Simmer 20 - 30 minutes.

Makes 4 quarts

Tip: Top with freshly grated Parmesan cheese when served.

Lima Bean Chowder

1 tablespoon olive oil
1/2 cup onion, chopped
1/2 pound ground venison
1/2 cup celery, chopped
1 cup carrots, chopped
1 bay leaf
1 can (14.5 ounces) diced
   tomatoes
1 can (15 ounces) lima beans,
   drained and rinsed
1 can (14 ounces) chicken
   broth
1/4 teaspoon garlic salt
1/4 teaspoon black pepper
1 teaspoon chicken base
1-1/2 teaspoons dried parsley
1/2 teaspoon Greek seasoning
Salt if needed

In a Dutch oven heat olive oil and sauté onion until tender. Add ground venison and cook until venison is browned. Add celery, carrots and bay leaf and sauté for 4 - 5 minutes. Add all the remaining ingredients, bring to a boil, reduce heat, cover and simmer for 30 minutes to blend flavors. Taste and adjust seasonings if needed.

Tips: Both the chicken broth and chicken base have lots of salt; therefore, we do not find additional salt is needed. If you like limas (and we do), you will love this lima bean and venison combination.

Two-Bean and Venison Sausage Soup

1 tablespoon olive oil
1/2 cup chopped onion
1 garlic clove, minced
1 pound venison kielbasa
   sausage, chopped into small
   cubes
1 can (14 ounces) chicken
   broth
1 cup water
1 teaspoon chicken base
1/4 teaspoon black pepper
1 package (9 ounces) frozen
   baby lima beans
1 can (16 ounces) Great
   Northern Beans, drained and
   rinsed
1 can (16 ounces) diced
   tomatoes, undrained
2 tablespoons grated Parmesan
   cheese

In a large sauce pan, heat olive oil and sauté onion until tender. Add garlic and sauté briefly. Then add chopped sausage, chicken broth, water, chicken base and lima beans. Bring to a boil, reduce heat and simmer for 15 minutes or until limas are tender. Add Great Northern Beans and diced tomatoes; return to a simmer to heat through. Serve soup sprinkled with Parmesan cheese.

Serves 4

Creamy Sausage and Potato Soup

1 tablespoon olive oil
1 pound ground venison bulk
  sausage
1 medium onion, chopped
16 ounces frozen hash brown
  potatoes (4 cups)
1 can (14.5 ounces) chicken
  broth
2 cups water
1 can (10.75 ounces) cream of
  celery soup, undiluted
1 can (10.75 ounces) cream of
  chicken soup, undiluted
2 cups milk
Garnish: shredded cheddar
  cheese

Heat oil in a large Dutch oven over medium heat and brown sausage, stirring until it crumbles and is no longer pink. Add onion and sauté until tender. Add potatoes, broth and water; bring to a boil, reduce heat, cover and simmer for 30 minutes. Stir in soups and milk; cook, stirring often, until thoroughly heat. Serve topped with cheddar cheese.

Tips: Since venison sausage is low fat, you can also use low-fat soups and skim milk for a lower-fat soup with a depth of flavor. Try pimento cheese sandwiches with this quick and easy soup.

Cabbage Soup

1/2 stick butter

2 large sweet onions, coarsely chopped

1 medium head cabbage, coarsely chopped

2 large containers (32 ounces each) chicken broth

1 teaspoon chicken base dissolved in 1 cup water

1/2 pound venison kielbasa, chopped

Salt (if needed) and freshly ground black pepper to taste

In a large Dutch oven, melt butter. Add onions and sauté until onions are limp. Add cabbage, broth, base and water, kielbasa and black pepper. Bring to a boil; reduce heat, cover, and simmer for 30 minutes or until cabbage is tender. Taste and adjust seasonings, if needed.

Tips: If desired, you can omit the chicken base and water; however, the base does add flavor and depth to the soup. The base is sold in jars and can be found at Sam's or Costco. Tone's is the brand we use. The base has lots more flavor than bouillon cubes. Black pepper enhances the cabbage, so use a heavy hand with it. If you like a bit more zip, add a few red pepper flakes. Be sure to taste before adding any salt because both the broth and base have salt in them.

Venison Barley Soup

2 tablespoons olive oil
1/2 cup onion, diced
1 garlic clove, minced
1 pound ground venison
1 can (14 ounces) chicken
 broth
2 cups water
1 cup celery, diced
1 cup potato, diced
1 cup carrots, cut into coins
3/4 - 1 teaspoon coarse salt
1/2 teaspoon freshly ground
 black pepper
1 teaspoon dried parsley
1/2 teaspoon dried basil
1 bay leaf
1/8 teaspoon thyme
1 can (16 ounces) diced
 tomatoes
2 tablespoons crushed sun-
 dried tomatoes
1 cup cooked barley

In a large soup kettle, heat the olive oil. Add onion and sauté until tender. Add minced garlic, stirring constantly for 1 minute. Add the ground venison and cook until browned. Add chicken broth, water, celery, potatoes, carrots, salt, pepper, parsley, basil, bay leaf and thyme. Bring to a boil. Reduce heat and simmer for 10 minutes or until vegetables are tender. Stir in the tomatoes with their juice, sun-dried tomatoes and cooked barley; simmer for another 10 minutes. Remove bay leaf and serve with garlic bread and garden salad.

Tips: Top off dinner with grilled pineapple with vanilla or rum raisin ice cream. Try using kosher or coarse salt. It dissolves easier and has more flavor; therefore, less salt is needed.

Italian Steak Soup

1 tablespoon olive oil
1/2 pound venison cubed steak,
  cut into thin strips (see tips)
1 medium onion, chopped
1 large garlic clove, minced
2 cans (14.5 ounces each) diced
  tomatoes
2 cups water
1 cup chopped carrots
1 zucchini squash, chopped
2 teaspoons beef base (see tips)
1 can (16 ounces) kidney
  beans, drained
1 can (14 ounces) Italian green
  beans, drained
1/2 teaspoon kosher salt
  (see tips)
1/2 teaspoon freshly ground
  black pepper
1 teaspoon dried Italian
  seasoning (see tips)
1/2 teaspoon dried oregano
1/2 teaspoon dried basil
Grated Parmesan cheese

Heat olive oil in a Dutch oven over medium-high heat and add steak. Brown on all sides quickly. Add onions and cook until tender. Add garlic and cook for 30 seconds, stirring constantly. Add all other ingredients and bring to a boil, reduce heat and simmer for 15 - 20 minutes or until carrots and venison are fork tender. Serve topped with grated Parmesan cheese.

Tips: Using smaller servings of lean meats and larger amounts of vegetables makes this a healthier soup. Ground venison can be used instead of the steak. If you package your cubed steak in one-pound containers, this is a great way to use half the container and reserve the remainder for another meal. Beef base (Tone's is the brand we prefer) is very similar to bouillon cubes, but the flavor is much more appealing. It is also high in sodium, so be sure to adjust the amount of salt you use. Kosher salt seems to have more flavor and dissolves easier. Also, using kosher salt has made it much easier for us to reduce our sodium intake. Crushing dried herbs and seasoning in the palm of your hand, or with a mortar and pestle, brings out the oils and flavors of the herbs. If you need to reduce your sodium intake, using more herbs is an easy way to add flavor.

Lentil and Kielbasa Soup

1/2 pound lentils
3 tablespoons olive oil
1 large sweet onion, chopped
2 garlic cloves, minced
1 cup chopped celery
1 cup chopped carrots
1 teaspoon dried thyme,
    crushed
1 teaspoon ground cumin
1/2 teaspoon kosher salt
3/4 teaspoon freshly ground
    black pepper
32 ounces chicken broth or
    homemade stock
1/4 cup tomato paste
1 cup water
1/4 cup sun-dried tomatoes,
    chopped
1/2 pound venison Kielbasa,
    chopped into 1/2-inch pieces
1 tablespoon red wine vinegar
Freshly grated Parmesan
    cheese

In a large bowl, cover the lentils with boiling water and allow to sit for 15 minutes. Drain well and set aside.

Heat olive oil in a large stockpot set over medium heat. Add onion and sauté for 5 minutes. Add garlic and continue to sauté for 1 minute. Add celery, carrots, thyme, cumin, salt and pepper and sauté another minute, stirring constantly. Add chicken broth, tomato paste (mixed with 1 cup water), lentils and dried tomatoes and bring to a boil. Cover, reduce heat and simmer until the lentils are cooked through, about 1 hour. Stir in the sausage and red wine vinegar and simmer until sausage is heated through, about 5 minutes more. Serve hot and sprinkle with Parmesan cheese.

Serves 6 - 8

Wild Rice and Venison Soup

1 tablespoon olive oil
1 small onion, diced
1 clove garlic, minced
1/2 pound ground venison
1 can (16 ounces) diced
   tomatoes
1 tablespoon tomato paste
3/4 teaspoon dried basil
1 can (14 ounces) chicken
   broth
1 cup cooked wild rice
Salt and pepper to taste

In a large sauce pan, sauté onion in olive oil until tender. Add garlic and sauté about 1 minute. Add ground venison and cook until no longer pink. Add tomatoes (with juice), tomato paste, basil, chicken broth, cooked rice, salt and freshly ground black pepper. Simmer about 10 minutes to blend flavors. Garnish with freshly grated Parmesan cheese.

Serves 4 - 6

Zucchini Soup

2 tablespoons olive oil
1/2 pound venison Italian
    sausage, casings removed
1 cup chopped celery
1/2 cup chopped onion
1/2 cup finely chopped carrots
2 medium zucchini, cut into
    1-inch pieces
3 cups lower-sodium chicken
    broth
28 ounces canned diced
    tomatoes
1/2 teaspoon sugar
1/4 teaspoon freshly ground
    black pepper
1/2 teaspoon dried Italian
    seasoning
1/2 teaspoon dried oregano
Salt to taste (if needed)
Grated Parmesan cheese

Heat olive oil over medium heat in a large Dutch oven, add sausage, which has casings removed and is broken into pieces. Brown about 5 minutes. Add celery, onion and carrots and cook 5 more minutes, stirring frequently. Stir in remaining ingredients, bring to a boil, reduce heat and simmer, covered, 15 minutes or until zucchini is tender. Serve topped with grated Parmesan cheese.

Tip: Even using lower-sodium chicken broth, we find that additional salt is not needed. Herbs help decrease the need for extra salt. For those with high blood pressure, this is a flavorful way to reduce your sodium intake for the day.

Taco Soup

1 pound ground venison
1 garlic clove, minced
1 medium onion, chopped
1 package (1.4 ounces) dry taco
   seasoning mix
1 can (15 ounces) stewed
   tomatoes
1 can (15 ounces) red kidney
   beans, rinsed and drained
1 can (16 ounces) corn, drained
1 can (10.5 ounces) beef broth
3 cups water

Tortilla chips
Sour cream
Grated cheese (try the Mexican
   blend)

Brown venison, garlic and onion. Add taco seasoning mix to venison and follow package instructions. In soup kettle, combine tomatoes, beans, corn, broth and water. Add venison mixture and let simmer for 30 minutes. To serve, divide crumbled tortilla chips between 6 - 8 soup bowls and add soup. Top with grated cheese and a dollop of sour cream.

Serves 6 - 8

Venison Noodle Soup

4 cups beef broth
1/4 – 1/2 pound noodles,
   broken
1/2 pound ground venison,
   browned
2 ribs celery
1 small onion, chopped
2 tablespoons margarine
Garlic salt to taste
Salt and pepper to taste
Chives and Parmesan cheese

Bring broth to a boil and cook noodles (spaghetti is fine). Brown venison. Sauté celery and onion in margarine. When noodles are done, add cooked venison, celery and onion. Add garlic salt, salt and pepper to taste. Simmer 10 - 15 minutes. Garnish with fresh chives and Parmesan cheese on top.

Tip: Leftover cooked burgers can be chopped and used in the soup.

Meatball Soup

1-1/2 pounds ground venison
1/2 cup fine bread crumbs
1 egg

6 cups beef broth or stock
1 cup sliced carrots
1 cup zucchini, cut into 1-inch
   chunks
1/2 cup chopped onion
1 cup chopped celery
1/3 cup long-grain rice
1 teaspoon salt
1/8 teaspoon black pepper
2 bay leaves
1/4 cup ketchup
2 cans (14 ounces each) Italian
   stewed tomatoes, undrained
   and chopped
1 can (8 ounces) tomato puree

Mix ground venison, bread crumbs and egg well. Shape into 1-inch balls and place in rectangular baking dish or pan (which has been coated with nonstick spray) 1/2 inch apart. Bake for 10-15 minutes at 400 degrees.

Put remaining ingredients in a 5-quart Dutch oven. Add cooked meatballs. Bring to a boil. Reduce heat; cover and simmer 1 hour or until vegetables and rice are tender.

Top soup with freshly grated cheese when served. Crusty French bread goes nicely with this soup.

Tip: A blender does a good job of making fine bread crumbs.

Vegetable and Venison Soup

2 large beef or ham bones
5-1/2 cups water
1 pound venison, cut into
   chunks
2 cans (16 ounces each) diced
   tomatoes
2 teaspoons salt
1 teaspoon black pepper
1 large onion, chopped
1 tablespoon Worcestershire
   sauce
5 medium carrots, thinly sliced
6 - 7 large ribs celery, chopped
5 - 6 medium potatoes, cubed
20 ounces frozen green beans
20 ounces frozen corn
10 ounces frozen lima beans
1/2 cup barley
1 teaspoon sugar
1/2 medium head cabbage,
   shredded

In a large soup pot, place bones, water, venison, tomatoes, salt, pepper and onion. Bring to a boil, reduce heat and simmer for 2 hours or until meat begins to fall apart. Remove soup bones and add all ingredients except cabbage. Cook until potatoes are tender. Add cabbage and cook until cabbage is tender. Serve with homemade corn bread or crusty French bread for a hearty meal.

Yield: 6 quarts

Tip: This soup makes such a large quantity that you may want to freeze several quarts for a quick heat-up dinner on one of those busy, hectic days.

Herbed White Bean and Sausage Soup

1-1/2 tablespoons olive oil
2 cups chopped onion
1 cup chopped carrots
2 teaspoons minced garlic
1 teaspoon dried basil
1 teaspoon dried thyme
1 teaspoon dried oregano
1 whole bay leaf
2 cups chopped, peeled
　　tomatoes
16 ounces dried navy beans
　　(see tip)
6 cups chicken stock (or water
　　and stock)
1 ham hock
1/2 pound browned, crumbled
　　venison bulk sausage
1 package (10 ounces) frozen
　　spinach, defrosted and
　　drained
Salt and pepper to taste

In a large soup pot over medium high heat, heat oil and sauté onions, carrots and garlic. Add dried herbs and bay leaf and sauté 1 minute. Add tomatoes, drained white beans, chicken stock or water, and ham hock. Bring to a boil. Lower heat and simmer until beans are tender (do not let liquid cook away completely; add more liquid if necessary) for about 1-1/2 hours.

Remove ham hock and chop ham. Return chopped ham and browned and crumbled venison sausage to soup. Add spinach and cook about 1 minute. Adjust salt and pepper seasonings. Serve immediately with hot homemade bread or bruschetta.

Tip: Beans can be soaked 6 - 8 hours or use the quick-soak method: Cover beans with cold water; bring to a boil; boil 2 minutes; cover, remove from heat and let stand 1 hour; drain and continue with recipe.

Steak and Veggie Soup

2 tablespoons olive oil
1 pound venison steak, cut into
    1-inch cubes
1/3 cup all-purpose flour
1 small onion, chopped
1 can (14 ounces) beef broth
2 cups water
1 teaspoon beef base
2 baking potatoes, cut into
    1/2-inch cubes
4 carrots, sliced
1 celery rib, chopped
1 package (10 ounces) frozen
    green peas, thawed
1 package (10 ounces) frozen
    corn, thawed
1 can (6 ounces) tomato paste
1 can (6 ounces) water (rinse
    out can and add)
1 teaspoon kosher salt, or to
    taste
1/2 teaspoon black pepper, or
    to taste

Toss steak cubes with flour. Brown floured steak in hot oil in a Dutch oven. Add onion and sauté until onion is tender. Add remaining ingredients, bring to a boil and simmer for 1 to 1-1/2 hours or until steak and potatoes are tender.

Tips: Hot corn muffins and slaw complete the meal. This soup does well in the slow cooker; just brown your steak, add all the other ingredients and cook on high for 6 - 8 hours or until vegetables and steak are tender.

Venison Chili with Beans

1 tablespoon olive oil
1 medium onion, chopped
1 clove garlic, minced
1 pound ground venison
1 can (14 ounces) diced
  tomatoes
1 can (8 ounces) tomato sauce
1 can (16 ounces) red kidney
  beans, drained
1/2 teaspoon kosher salt
1-1/2 to 2 teaspoons chili
  powder (as desired)
1/4 – 1/2 teaspoon cumin
1/2 cup sun-dried tomatoes
1 bay leaf

Heat olive oil in a large skillet; sauté onion until golden, add garlic and cook for 30 seconds, add venison and cook until browned. Stir in tomatoes, tomato sauce, kidney beans, sun-dried tomatoes and seasonings. Bring to a simmer, reduce heat and simmer for 1 hour. Remove bay leaf. Serve with crackers, tortilla chips or crusty bread.

Serves 4

Tips: Leftover chili and grits make a delicious, hearty breakfast for those early morning hunts. Some possible toppings for chili are: chopped onions, grated cheddar cheese, chili powder, avocado slices, sour cream, olives, bell peppers, hard-boiled eggs, cilantro, parsley, grated jalapeño cheese, crushed chili pepper pods, croutons, tortilla chips, popcorn and fried egg.

Northern Chili

2 pounds ground (or chopped)
  venison
2 tablespoons canola oil
1 cup chopped onion
1 can (6 ounces) tomato paste
1 teaspoon cinnamon
1 teaspoon black pepper
1/2 teaspoon cayenne pepper
1/2 teaspoon ground cumin
1/2 teaspoon ground allspice
2 tablespoons Worcestershire
  sauce
2 teaspoons salt
1 tablespoon vinegar
1 bay leaf
1 cup red wine

In a large kettle, brown the venison in oil with the onion; add the tomato paste, cinnamon, black pepper, cayenne, cumin, allspice, Worcestershire sauce, salt, vinegar, bay leaf, wine and 2 cups water. Bring the mixture to a boil. Simmer the chili, stirring occasionally, for 1 hour; add an additional cup of water and simmer the chili, stirring occasionally for 2 hours more. Discard the bay leaf.

Serves 6 - 8

Tip: Some people prefer their chili without beans; this is one to try.

Chili in the Crockpot

2 pounds ground (or chopped)
   venison
1 medium onion, diced
1 cup fresh sliced mushrooms
1 garlic clove, minced
1 bell pepper, chopped
   (optional)
2 ribs celery, chopped
2 tablespoons canola oil
2 cans (16 ounces each) kidney
   beans, rinsed and drained
2 cans (16 ounces each)
   tomatoes, undrained
1-1/2 tablespoons sugar
1 tablespoon Worcestershire
   sauce
1 package chili seasonings
   (or 1-1/2 to 2 tablespoons
   chili powder)
1 - 3 cups water
Salt and pepper to taste

Brown venison, onion, mushrooms, garlic, bell pepper and celery in oil. Place in crockpot and add all other ingredients. Mix well; cook on medium for 6 - 8 hours.

Tip: Uncle Buck's Chili Seasoning is one of our favorites.

Quick and Simple Chili

1 - 2 pounds ground or
    chopped venison
1 large onion, chopped
1 can (14 ounces) tomatoes,
    diced
1 can (16 ounces) rinsed and
    drained beans, kidney or
    pinto
1 can (6 ounces) tomato paste
1 cup water
1 package chili seasoning
Salt and pepper to taste

Brown venison and onion. Add
tomatoes, drained and rinsed
beans, tomato paste, water and
seasonings. Simmer 45 minutes or
longer for flavors to blend. Serve
hot, topped with grated cheese and
chives.

*Tips: Substitute taco seasoning for chili seasoning and go Mexican
with tacos or burritos. Using the pre-packaged seasoning mixes is easy;
however, we like to add our own seasonings (chili powder, garlic, red
pepper and/or cumin) instead of using a mix. That makes it easy to
add only the flavors we like and to adjust the "heat" accordingly.*

Beer Chili

1 - 2 tablespoons olive oil
1 medium onion, finely
   chopped
2 garlic cloves, minced
1-1/2 pounds ground venison
1 can (28 ounces) diced
   tomatoes with juice
1 bottle (or 2 cups) beer
2 - 3 tablespoons chili powder
1-1/2 teaspoons ground cumin
1 bay leaf
1 can (16 ounces) kidney
   beans, drained and rinsed
1 teaspoon kosher salt, or to
   taste
1/2 teaspoon black pepper, or
   to taste

Heat olive oil in a Dutch oven over medium heat. Add chopped onion and sauté until the onions are tender (about 5 minutes). Add garlic and sauté 1 minute, stirring constantly. Add ground venison and cook until brown, breaking it apart as you go. If your ground venison is very lean, you may need to add an additional tablespoon of oil. Add the tomatoes, beer, chili powder, cumin, bay leaf, kidney beans, salt and pepper. Simmer for 30 - 45 minutes or until chili has thickened slightly. Garnish as desired. Some options are: chopped green onions, grated cheddar cheese or sour cream.

Tips: The flavor of the beer really comes through in this chili. Corn bread is a nice accompaniment to chili.

Stove Top Venison Stew

1-1/2 to 2 pounds venison stew
   meat
2 tablespoons olive oil
1 medium onion, chopped
2 garlic cloves, minced
1 can (14 ounces) beef broth
2 bay leaves
2 - 3 medium potatoes, peeled
   and chopped
1/2 cup sliced mushrooms
1 cup chopped carrots
1/2 cup chopped celery
1 can (11 ounces) cream of
   mushroom soup
1 tablespoon tomato paste
1 cup frozen green peas
Freshly ground black pepper to
   taste

Sear venison cubes in hot olive oil until lightly browned. Remove venison from pan. Sauté onions until tender; add garlic and sauté briefly (about 1 minute). Add beef broth and one can water. Stir to get browned bits from bottom of pan. Return venison to pan, add bay leaves and bring to a simmer. Cover and simmer until almost tender. Add potatoes, mushrooms, carrots and celery and simmer until potatoes are tender. Add mushroom soup, 1 tablespoon tomato paste and peas. Simmer until heated through and season with black pepper. Remove bay leaves. Serve with crusty bread and red wine.

Tips: Do not add salt until tested. Canned soups and broths are high in sodium. When I open a can of tomato paste, I freeze the remainder in tablespoon-sized servings (individually wrapped and placed in freezer bag) and it is ready for my next recipe.

Simple Oven Stew

1/4 cup flour
1/2 teaspoon salt
1/4 teaspoon black pepper
2 pounds venison stew meat,
   cut into 1-inch pieces
3 - 4 tablespoons canola oil
4 - 5 medium potatoes, peeled,
   cut into chunks
4 - 5 carrots, cut into chunks
2 ribs celery, cut into chunks
1 package Lipton dry onion
   soup mix
3 cups water

Mix flour, salt and pepper in a paper bag. Add venison and shake well. Brown meat in oil and place in a large casserole. Add potatoes, carrots, celery, soup and water. Cover and cook at 325 degrees for 2 hours or until meat and vegetables are tender.

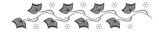

Crockpot Onion and Venison Stew

1 pound venison stew meat
3 - 4 medium potatoes,
   chopped
1 medium onion, chopped
2 carrots, chopped
2 ribs celery, chopped
1 cup fresh sliced mushrooms
1 can onion soup (more or less
   can be used; barely cover the
   chopped ingredients)
1/2 soup can water
1/2 can wine
Black pepper to taste
1 package (5 ounces) green
   peas

Place chopped ingredients in crockpot and cover with onion soup, water and wine. Use enough soup to barely cover meat and vegetables. Cook on medium about 6 hours or until meat and vegetables are tender. Add peas and thickening if desired and increase heat to high. Cook until peas are tender and stew has thickened. Thicken stew with a slurry (1/4 cup water and 2 tablespoons flour mixed well) if desired. Serve with hot sourdough bread.

Tip: Try duck or rabbit in this stew.

Venison and Squirrel Stew

1 pound venison, cubed
2 squirrels
3 - 4 chicken pieces (legs or thighs)
1 cup sliced celery
1 medium onion, chopped
Salt and pepper to taste
1 can (46 ounces) tomato juice
1 package (10 ounces) frozen corn
1 package (10 ounces) frozen green beans
4 medium potatoes, cubed
3 carrots, chopped
1 package (10 ounces) frozen green peas

Combine venison, squirrel, chicken, celery, onion, salt and pepper. Cover with water. Cook until meat is almost tender. Add tomato juice, corn, green beans, potatoes, carrots and peas. Cook until tender. Remove bones and serve with hot bread.

Serves 6 - 8

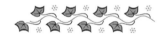

Sauerbraten

2 pounds venison, cut into chunks
1 can (10.75 ounces) beef broth
1/3 cup brown sugar
1/3 cup cider vinegar
1/2 cup finely chopped onion
3/4 cups water
10 - 12 ginger snaps, crushed

Place all ingredients except ginger snaps in crockpot and cook on high about 6 hours or until venison is tender. Add crushed ginger snaps and stir until thickened.

Serves 6 - 8

Venison Osso Bucco

2 tablespoons olive oil
3 pounds venison roast, cut 1-
1/2-inches thick
1/2 teaspoon kosher salt
1/4 teaspoon freshly ground
black pepper
1 medium onion, chopped
1 medium carrot, diced
1 medium celery rib, diced
1/2 cup dry white wine
1 can (15 ounces) tomatoes in
juice, drained and chopped
(1/2 cup juice reserved)
1 can (14 ounces) beef broth
1 teaspoon beef base
1/2 teaspoon dried basil
1/2 teaspoon dried rosemary
1/4 teaspoon dried thyme
2 bay leaves

In a Dutch oven, heat 1 tablespoon of oil over medium-high heat. In batches, add the venison and cook until lightly browned. Transfer meat to a platter and season with salt and pepper.

Heat remaining tablespoon of oil. Add the onion, carrot, celery and garlic and cook, stirring occasionally until softened (about 3 minutes). Stir in the wine and cook until almost evaporated. Add the tomatoes, reserved juice, broth, beef base and herbs. Return the venison to the Dutch oven and bring to a boil, cover, reduce heat and simmer for 2 to 2-1/2 hours until fork tender. Be sure to taste and adjust seasonings. Remove lid during the last 30 minutes for the sauce to thicken. Meanwhile, make a gremolata by combining 2 tablespoons chopped fresh parsley, grated zest of 1 lemon and 1 minced garlic clove in a small bowl.

Arrange the venison on a deep serving platter and pour the sauce over the venison. Sprinkle with gremolata and serve with rice or pasta.

Serves 6 - 8

Norwegian Venison Goulash

3 pounds venison
1/2 cup flour
4 tablespoons butter
1 cup chopped onion
2 garlic cloves, minced
2 teaspoon salt, or to taste
1 tablespoon paprika
1 cup dry red wine
1 can (8 ounces) tomato sauce
1-1/2 cups beef broth
1 cup sour cream

Pound venison lightly, sprinkle with flour and pound again. Cut venison into 1 - 2-inch cubes.

Melt butter in a Dutch oven and sauté the onions about 10 minutes. Add garlic and sauté briefly. Add the venison and brown on all sides. Mix in the salt, paprika, wine, tomato sauce and broth. Cover and cook over low heat for 2 to 2-1/2 hours or until venison is tender. Stir in sour cream just before serving. Serve over egg noodles, dumplings or spaetzle.

Serves 6 - 8

Tip: Adding the garlic after sautéing the onions prevents the garlic from developing a bitter taste.

Quick and Easy Ground Venison Goulash

8 ounces elbow macaroni,
   cooked according to package
   directions
1 tablespoon olive oil
1/2 cup chopped onion
1 garlic clove, finely minced
1 pound ground venison
1/2 teaspoon ground cumin
2-1/2 teaspoons Hungarian
   paprika
Pinch ground nutmeg
1/4 – 1/2 teaspoon dried
   marjoram
Salt and black pepper to taste
1 can (14 ounces) diced
   tomatoes, undrained
2 rounded tablespoons sour
   cream
Chopped fresh parsley

While the macaroni is cooking, heat olive oil over medium-high heat in a deep skillet. Add onion and sauté until tender. Add garlic and sauté 1 minute. Add ground venison, stirring and crumbling while browning. Add seasonings; mix in tomatoes and cooked macaroni. Heat through and then stir in sour cream. Garnish with parsley and serve immediately.

Serves 3 - 4

Tip: Most stew-type dishes take a long time to prepare, but as the title suggests, this one is quickly and easily prepared.

German-Style Venison Stew

2 tablespoons olive oil, divided
1 to 1-1/2 pounds venison stew
  meat, cut into small chunks
1 cup onion, chopped
1/2 anchovy
1 garlic clove, minced
1 large apple, peeled and
  shredded
1 large carrot, shredded
1 cup water
1 teaspoon beef base
  (or bouillon cube)
1/3 cup red wine
  (such as merlot)
1 bay leaf
1/8 teaspoon dried thyme,
  crushed
1/4 – 1/2 teaspoon salt
4 cups noodles, cooked and
  drained
1/4 teaspoon poppy seeds

Heat 1 tablespoon olive oil in a Dutch oven until hot. Add venison chunks; do not turn venison but allow to sear and brown quickly on one side before turning. If meat is crowded in the pan, it will not brown, but will steam; therefore, brown the venison in two batches. Remove venison from pan. Add and heat another tablespoon of olive oil, reduce heat slightly, add onions and anchovy and cook until onions are golden and anchovy has dissolved. Add garlic and sauté briefly. Add apple, carrot, water, beef base, wine, bay leaf and thyme. Bring to a boil, reduce heat and simmer, covered, for 1-1/2 to 2 hours or until venison is tender. Remove lid during last 30 minutes of simmering to thicken stew. Remove bay leaf and serve stew over poppy-seed noodles.

Serves 4

Venison Burgundy in the Slow Cooker

1 to 1-1/2 pounds venison stew
   meat
2 tablespoons beefy dry onion
   soup mix
1/2 cup chopped onions
1 garlic clove, minced
1/4 teaspoon kosher salt
1/4 teaspoon freshly ground
   black pepper
1 bay leaf
1 cup fresh mushrooms, sliced
1 cup red wine (medium dry)
1/2 cup water

Place all ingredients in slow cooker and cook on medium for 8-9 hours. Remove bay leaf before serving and adjust seasonings if needed. Serve over fluffy rice.

Serves 3 - 4

Tip: For an added layer of flavor, dredge venison in seasoned flour and brown in oil before adding to slow cooker.

Venison and Cherry Stew

1 pound venison stew meat

Marinade:

1 cup dry white wine
3 tablespoons olive oil
1/2 medium onion, sliced
1/2 teaspoon dried thyme
1 bay leaf
2 slices bacon, cut into a small dice
1/2 medium onion, chopped
1/4 cup flour
1 garlic clove, minced
1 can (14 ounces) beef broth
1 can (14.5 ounces) Red Tart Pie Cherries in water
1/8 teaspoon rosemary
1/8 teaspoon thyme
1 bay leaf

Freshly ground black pepper to taste
Salt to taste

Combine wine, oil, onion, thyme and bay leaf in a resealable plastic bag. Add venison cubes and marinate 24 hours in the refrigerator. Drain venison well, remove onion and pat the meat dry with paper towels. Discard onion and marinade.

Fry the bacon in a Dutch oven over moderate heat until almost crisp; remove from pan with a slotted spoon. Add chopped onion to bacon drippings and cook until tender, about 3 minutes. Remove from pan with a slotted spoon. Add some additional oil if there is not enough bacon grease to brown venison. Dredge the venison in flour, shaking off excess flour, and add venison and brown on all sides. Add garlic and cook until fragrant, about 1 minute. Return onion and bacon to pan. Add beef broth, juice drained from cherries, rosemary, thyme, bay leaf, black pepper and salt. Bring to a boil, reduce heat, cover and simmer until venison is tender (about 2 hours). Remove lid during last 30 minutes to thicken stew. If needed, add a slurry of water and flour to thicken. Add cherries during last 15 minutes of cooking. Taste and adjust seasonings.

Serves 3 - 4

Chapter 6

Unusual Approaches: Sausage, Organ Meats, Jerky and More

Sadly, many folks for whom venison forms a key dietary item fail to realize just how versatile the meat can be. Thoughts of a breakfast with some sausage patties, a tailgating party with brats or kielbasa, or for those of a Southern persuasion (as we are), a meal with grits and venison sausage gravy are enough to put the salivary glands working at warp speed. Moreover, there are so many kinds of sausage, and so many ways to make each kind, that you could make a staunch argument for turning an entire season's taking of venison into such delicacies (and some folks we know do just that). For those wanting to take a bit of extra trouble and willing to invest in some basic equipment, producing link sausages of all kinds lies well within the realm of possibility.

Then there are the most wasted parts of the deer – organ meats. If you enjoy liver, occasionally dine on scrapple, eat organ meats from commercially reared animals or simply are one of those individuals who clings to the credo of "waste not, want not," then the ways we offer to prepare organ meats merit your attention. Taking matters a step further, organ meats actually are less trouble than the rest of the deer. Once you have field dressed the deer and removed the heart, liver and possibly kidneys, you don't have to worry about aging the meat. When washed, cleaned and sliced, it is ready for preparation. It is also worth noting that with organ meats from deer, unlike those from domestic animals, you don't have to worry about the animal's internal filtering system having been exposed to all sorts of antibiotics, supplements and the like.

Nor should other uses of venison, from the ever-popular jerky to really offbeat approaches, be overlooked. It is particularly satisfying to chew on a piece of jerky from a previous hunt while sitting in the stand on another hunt, and for those with a deeply rooted sense of history, carrying some when afield or on a long hike takes the mind along in a pleasure journey of time travel. Jerky and its first cousin, pemmican, were foods of convenience for hardy frontiersmen and the mountain men, and to walk in the footsteps of these intrepid adventurers, with tasty products of your own hunting providing the medium, is to tred trails of wonder.

Creamed Leeks with Sausage

1 tablespoon olive oil
1/2 pound venison bulk
 sausage, mild
3 large leeks
3 tablespoons butter
1 garlic clove, minced
1 cup fat-free half and half
Pinch of nutmeg
Salt and black pepper to taste

1/2 cup soft bread crumbs
2 tablespoons butter, melted

Heat olive oil in a skillet and fry sausage over medium heat until browned and crumbled. Set aside.

Trim the leeks of all but about 2 inches of the green tops. Slice the leeks down the middle, and rinse the layers thoroughly under cold water to remove all grit. Take care with the rinsing, as there tends to be lots of hidden grit in leeks. Slice the leeks crosswise at 1-inch intervals.

Preheat oven to 425 degrees. In a large, heavy sauce pan, melt the 3 tablespoons of butter over medium heat; add the garlic and stir for 1 minute. Add the leeks and cook, stirring often, until they have wilted, about 5 - 7 minutes. Add the half and half and nutmeg, season with salt and pepper, and cook until the leeks are tender, 8 - 10 minutes.

Pour the leeks mixture into a shallow baking dish, spoon the sausage over the top, sprinkle bread crumbs over sausage and drizzle with remaining 2 tablespoons melted butter. Bake until golden brown and bubbly, about 10 - 15 minutes. Serve hot.

Serves 4

Tips: We use olive oil to cook our sausage because we have only 10 percent fat added. Sausage with a higher fat content may not require the use of the olive oil. If your sausage is hot and spicy, it will dominate the leeks; therefore, we prefer a milder sausage. Be meticulous rinsing the leeks because lots of grit gets inside the sections. If the leeks mixture does not thicken enough, you can thicken it with a slurry of equal parts flour and water mixed well and added to the leeks mixture. It will not thicken until the mixture is brought up to a boil, however. This makes a different and impressive side dish, but it is also great for a simple meal with a salad, good bread and wine.

Southern-Style Spicy Corn Bread with Sausage

1 tablespoon olive oil
1 pound venison bulk sausage
1 cup diced onion

1 cup white cornmeal
1/2 cup all-purpose flour
1 teaspoon salt
1/2 teaspoon baking soda
2 eggs, slightly beaten
1 cup buttermilk
1/2 cup canola oil
1 can (15 ounces) black-eyed
    peas, drained and rinsed
2 cups shredded cheddar
    cheese
3/4 cup cream-style corn
1 can (4.5 ounces) chopped
    green chiles

Heat olive oil in a large skillet over medium heat and cook sausage and onion until sausage crumbles and is no longer pink. Drain, if needed, and set aside.

In a large mixing bowl, combine cornmeal, flour, salt and baking soda; mix with a whisk and make a well in the center.

Stir together eggs, buttermilk and oil. Add to dry ingredients; stir until moistened. Batter will not be smooth. Add sausage and onion mixture, peas, cheese, corn and chiles to batter; stir well to blend.

Pour into a greased 9 x 13-inch baking dish and bake at 350 degrees for 1 hour or until golden brown.

Serve with a green salad for a main dish or as an appetizer when cut into small squares.

Serves 6

Tips: Do not use the olive oil if your sausage has more than 10 percent fat. Spice the corn bread up by using hot venison sausage and perhaps adding some jalapeño peppers. This is a meal in one dish, and a green salad compliments it.

Virginia's Brunch Casserole

1 - 2 pounds venison bulk
   sausage
1/2 cup chopped onion
1 cup sliced mushrooms

2 cups milk
4 eggs, slightly beaten
3 cups grated sharp cheddar
   cheese
1 teaspoon dry mustard
1 teaspoon onion powder
1 teaspoon Worcestershire
   sauce

8 slices bread, crust cut off and
   cut into strips

1 can (10.75 ounces) cream of
   mushroom soup
1/3 cup milk
Paprika

In a large skillet over medium heat, cook sausage, onion and mushrooms; drain well, if needed, and set aside.

In a large bowl, combine the sausage mixture, milk, eggs, cheese, dry mustard, onion powder and Worcestershire. Butter a 9 x 13-inch pan and line it with strips of bread. Pour sausage and egg mixture over bread and refrigerate over night.

Combine the mushroom soup and milk and pour over the casserole. Sprinkle with paprika and bake, uncovered, at 325 degrees for 1-1/2 hours or until set.

Biscuit Cups

1 can (6 ounces) buttermilk
biscuits (5 biscuits)

1/4 – 1/2 pound venison bulk
sausage

1 tablespoon cream cheese

1 tablespoon sour cream

1 tablespoon chives

1/4 cup egg beaters (or real
eggs)

1/4 cup Asiago cheese (or
Parmesan cheese)

Brown sausage; drain and
crumble. Press biscuit dough into
greased muffin tins. Put sausage in
cups and top with cheese.

Mix softened cream cheese, sour
cream, chives and egg beaters;
pour slowly over cups and bake at
350 degrees for 20 - 25 minutes or
until golden brown and egg
mixture has set.

Makes 5

*Tip: If you have large muffin tins, use them instead of the regular-size
ones because you can get more sausage and egg per cup in proportion
to the amount of biscuit.*

Cheesy Sausage Roll

1 pound venison bulk sausage
  or venison Italian sausage
1/2 cup sliced mushrooms
1 teaspoon Italian seasoning
1/2 teaspoon salt
1 can (10 ounces) pizza dough
2 cups shredded mozzarella
  cheese
1/2 cup grated Parmesan
  cheese
1 egg white, beaten

Preheat oven to 350 degrees. Spray a cookie sheet with Pam.

Cook sausage and mushrooms, stirring to crumble. Add seasonings and drain well if needed. Shape pizza dough into a rectangle on a floured surface. Spread sausage over dough. Sprinkle mozzarella and Parmesan cheeses over sausage. Roll up jelly-roll style. Place on prepared cookie sheet seam side down. Beat egg white and brush over dough. Bake until golden brown, about 20 minutes. Slice and serve warm.

Serves 4 - 6

Tips: Putting the crust on waxed or parchment paper to form into a rectangle makes rolling the crust easier; however, be sure to flour the paper to prevent crust from sticking. This makes a nice accompaniment to soup but can be used as an appetizer or party food also.

Meatball Subs

Meatballs:

1/2 pound ground venison
1/2 pound bulk venison
  sausage
1/2 cup Parmesan cheese
1/4 cup milk
1 cup soft bread crumbs
1/4 cup finely chopped onions
1 egg, beaten
1/2 teaspoon garlic salt
1/4 teaspoon black pepper
1/4 teaspoon dried basil
1/4 teaspoon dried oregano
1 tablespoon dried parsley
1/4 teaspoon lemon juice

Sauce:

2 tablespoons olive oil
1/2 large red onion, sliced and
  divided
1/2 cup sliced fresh
  mushrooms
1/2 large green bell pepper, cut
  into thin strips (optional)
1/4 teaspoon sugar
1 jar (14 ounces) prepared
  meatless spaghetti sauce

4 hoagie rolls, split
1 cup shredded mozzarella
  cheese

Lightly mix all meatball ingredients. Be gentle and handle the meatballs as little as possible for best results. Shape into 1-inch meatballs and place on a cookie sheet. Place in a freezer to get meatballs very cold before cooking (about 10 minutes).

In a large skillet, heat two tablespoons olive oil and add onion, mushrooms and peppers. Sauté until the vegetables are tender. Sprinkle 1/4 teaspoon sugar over veggies, stir well and remove from the pan. Add meatballs (which have been chilled thoroughly) to pan and sauté until brown and no longer pink in the center (about 15 minutes). Turn meatballs gently to keep from breaking up. Add spaghetti sauce and vegetables to meatballs and simmer 5 - 8 minutes until all ingredients are hot.

Split hoagie rolls, place on a baking sheet and sprinkle with mozzarella cheese. Bake at 400 degrees until cheese melts (about 5 minutes). Spoon meatballs and sauce over rolls. Serve immediately.

Serves 4

Tip: To make soft bread crumbs, place torn bread slices in blender container and pulse on and off until bread is fine crumbs. Two slices of bread makes about 1 cup soft bread crumbs.

Broccoli Casserole

3 slices bread
1/2 pound venison bulk
  sausage
1 package (10 ounces) frozen
  broccoli, thawed
1 cup shredded sharp cheddar
  cheese
3 eggs
1 cup milk
1/2 teaspoon dry mustard
1/4 teaspoon salt
1/8 teaspoon nutmeg
Several dashes black pepper

Cut bread into cubes and place in a greased 8 x 8-inch baking dish. Cook sausage in a skillet until browned. Spoon over bread. Place broccoli between paper towels to remove water and then place on top of sausage. Spread cheese evenly over broccoli.

In a small bowl, beat together eggs, milk, mustard, salt, nutmeg and pepper. Pour mixture in baking dish. Bake in a 350-degree oven for 35 - 40 minutes or until a knife inserted in the center comes out clean.

Serves 4

Tips: This casserole can be assembled the night before and refrigerated. Uncover and bake 40 - 45 minutes. Try this dish for a Sunday brunch, supper or lunch with a green salad alongside. Venison and pork sausages can be mixed for added flavor.

Apple and Sausage Sandwich

1/2 pound venison bulk
  sausage
2 tablespoons butter
1/2 large Granny Smith apple,
  sliced thinly and cored
2 slices toast
Several pinches sugar
Sprinkling of cinnamon sugar

Melt butter in frying pan over medium heat. Make flat patties of sausage and cook in butter until the center is no longer pink. Remove from pan. Place apples in pan and sprinkle with a pinch of sugar and dash of cinnamon sugar. Brown apples slightly, turn and sprinkle with another pinch of sugar and dash of cinnamon sugar. Cook until slightly tender. Place apples on toast and top with sausage patties. Serve open-faced sandwiches immediately.

Serves 2

Tip: Venison sausage is very lean, so the butter adds flavor and gives drippings for cooking the apples.

Italian Sausage and Spinach Roll

1/2 pound mild venison Italian sausage, cooked, drained and chopped
1 cup mushrooms
1 package (10 ounces) frozen, chopped spinach, thawed and patted dry
1 cup shredded mozzarella cheese
1 egg, separated
2 garlic cloves, minced
2 packages (10 ounces each) refrigerated pizza crust
1 can (8 ounces) pizza sauce

Preheat oven to 400 degrees.

Chop cooked sausage and mushrooms; place in a large bowl and add spinach and cheese.

In a small bowl, separate egg; add yolk to spinach mixture, reserving egg white.

Mince garlic and mix with spinach mixture. Roll one pizza crust into a 12 x 9-inch rectangle; spoon half of spinach mixture over dough to within 1/2 inch of edges of dough. Starting at the longest side of rectangle, roll up dough, jelly-roll style; press seam together to seal. Repeat with remaining pizza crust and filling. Place rolls, seam sides down on a 15-inch baking stone or pizza pan. Join ends of rolls to form 1 large ring; pinch together to seal. Brush lightly beaten egg white onto dough. Bake 25 - 30 minutes.

Heat pizza sauce and spoon over servings.

Apple Quiche

1/2 pound venison bulk
  sausage
1/2 cup onion, chopped
1/8 teaspoon thyme
1-1/2 cups apples, cut into
  cubes
1 tablespoon lemon juice
1 tablespoon brown sugar
1/3 cup dried cherries
1/2 cup grated cheese
2 eggs
1/2 cup egg beaters
2 cups half and half or light
  cream
1 pie shell

Cook sausage, onion and thyme until sausage is browned; drain if needed. In a bowl, toss apples with lemon juice and sugar. Add sausage mixture, cherries, cheese, eggs, egg beaters and cream. Mix well. Bake in a large pie shell at 350 degrees for 1 hour or until the center is set and does not shake.

Tip: This makes a large pie, so I used an 8-inch square casserole dish lined with pie crust.

Hearty Baked Beans

1/2 - 1 pound venison bulk
  sausage
1 onion, chopped
4 cups undrained canned pork
  and beans
1 cup drained canned lima
  beans
1 cup drained canned kidney
  beans
1/2 cup brown sugar (or
  pancake syrup)
1 cup ketchup
2 tablespoons mustard
2 teaspoons Worcestershire
  sauce
1/2 teaspoon chili powder
  (optional)
4 slices bacon

Crumble sausage and cook until no longer pink. Add onion before sausage is completely done and cook until onion is tender crisp. If you have any fat, drain well. Add all other ingredients, except bacon, and mix well. Place in a 9 x 13-inch baking dish, top with bacon slices and bake at 350 degrees for about 1 hour until beans are as thick as you desire.

Tips: This is good for cookouts, buffets or covered-dish dinners. This can also be cooked in the crockpot on low for about 4 hours. For variation, ground venison can be substituted for the sausage.

Sausage Gravy

2 tablespoons margarine or
  butter
3/4 - 1 cup cooked,
  crumbled venison sausage
  (1/2 - 3/4 pound uncooked)
2 tablespoons flour
1 cup milk
1 teaspoon Worcestershire
  sauce
Salt and pepper to taste

Melt margarine in a skillet. Add cooked sausage and stir to break up and heat through. Add flour and cook about 1 minute. Add milk and Worcestershire sauce. Season to taste. Cook until thickened and serve over toast or hot biscuits.

Serves 2

Tip: This is a good way to use leftover sausage; however, if no leftovers are available, you can just cook your sausage, and then add the margarine and flour and continue as above.

Red Beans and Rice

1 cup regular, long-grain rice
2 tablespoons olive oil
1 cup chopped celery
2 garlic cloves, minced
1 cup chopped sweet onion
1/2 teaspoon dried thyme
1/2 teaspoon dried oregano
1/2 teaspoon dried parsley
1 bay leaf
1 can (15 ounces) rinsed,
    drained red kidney beans
1/4 cup chopped ham
1 cup cooked venison bulk
    sausage, crumbled and
    drained
1 cup low-salt chicken broth
1/2 teaspoon Worcestershire
    sauce
Salt and black pepper to taste
Hot pepper sauce to taste

Prepare rice as directed on label and keep warm. Meanwhile, in a 3-quart pan, heat oil and add celery, garlic and onion. Cook until tender crisp; add herbs, rinsed and drained beans, ham, cooked sausage, chicken broth and Worcestershire sauce. Simmer 10 - 15 minutes. Season to taste and serve over hot rice.

Tip: The flavor of the herbs decreases the need for salt.

Fresh Ground Sausage

1 pound ground venison
1 pound ground pork (such as
　Boston Butt)
2 teaspoons fennel seed
1 teaspoon garlic powder
1/2 - 1 teaspoons crushed red
　pepper flakes
1/2 teaspoon sweet paprika
2 teaspoons salt
1/4 – 1/2 teaspoon black
　pepper

Combine all ingredients in a large bowl; mix well. Shape into patties and cook in a nonstick skillet over medium heat for 10 - 12 minutes or until meat is no longer pink in the center. Turn patties over only once or twice while cooking.

Serves 8

Tips: Patties can be frozen in resealable freezer bags between layers of wax paper. To prepare from frozen state, cook patties in a nonstick skillet over medium-low heat until meat is no longer pink in the center (about 20 minutes), turning patties over twice. For an even quicker sausage recipe, Penzey's Spices has a delicious venison sausage spice and herb blend that can be added to ground venison for a tasty sausage.

Venison Hash Omelet

2 tablespoons butter
1 small onion, finely chopped
2 cups diced, cooked venison
2 slices bacon, cooked and
   crumbled
3 eggs, lightly beaten
Salt and pepper to taste

Melt butter in a large skillet. Add onion and sauté until tender; stir in cooked venison and bacon to heat through. Add eggs and spread in pan; season if desired. Let bottom brown like omelet. Fold over and serve.

Serves 2

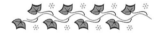

Hash Brown Potatoes with Venison

1/2 stick margarine or butter
1 small onion, diced
1/2 small bell pepper, chopped
   (optional)
1 garlic clove, minced
1 pound cooked venison, diced
   very small
4 medium potatoes, cooked
   and diced
Salt and pepper to taste
Few dashes Tabasco

Melt margarine in a large skillet; add onion, bell pepper and garlic and cook until tender. Add venison and potatoes. Season to taste. Mix and fry until browned. Sometimes you may need to add more margarine. Serve when browned. Top with ketchup. Serve along with eggs and toast for a hearty breakfast.

Jerky

1-1/2 pounds venison, partially frozen

Marinade:

1/4 cup Worcestershire sauce
1/4 cup soy sauce
1 teaspoon liquid smoke
1 teaspoon onion powder
1/2 teaspoon garlic powder
1/4 teaspoon black pepper
Several dashes hot sauce (such as Tabasco)

Partially freeze venison and slice into 1/4-inch pieces. Mix marinade ingredients and add venison slices; marinate 16 - 24 hours in a refrigerator.

Cover bottom rack of oven with foil. Place strips of venison on top rack. Set oven temperature at 150 degrees and crack door slightly. By cracking the door, temperature will be between 130 and 140 degrees (at 150 degrees the jerky tends to be too crunchy). Dry jerky for 6 - 8 hours. Store in airtight containers.

Tip: Partially freezing the venison makes slicing thinly much easier.

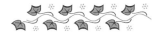

Party Pâté

2 pounds venison, cooked
1 medium onion, chopped
1 garlic clove, minced
1 hard-boiled egg
1/2 cup mayonnaise (good quality, such as Hellman's)
1 stick butter, softened (do not substitute)
1/4 cup bourbon (high quality)
1/2 teaspoon salt, or to taste
1/4 teaspoon freshly ground black pepper, or to taste
1 bay leaf
Chives for garnish

Place venison, onion, garlic, and egg in food processor and pulse until smooth. Add mayonnaise and softened butter and mix only enough to thoroughly blend. Add bourbon, salt and pepper and blend well. Mold into a ball and top with bay leaf. Wrap securely with plastic wrap and refrigerate over night. Remove bay leaf, garnish with chives and serve with Melba toast, party rye or assorted crackers.

Croquettes

2 slices bacon, chopped and
  cooked
1/4 cup finely chopped onion
1-1/2 to 2 cups finely chopped
  cooked venison
1/2 cup cooked, crumbled pork
  sausage
1 tablespoon currant jelly
1 teaspoon dry mustard
1 egg, slightly beaten
Salt and pepper to taste

Coating:

2 eggs, beaten
Flour
Fine bread crumbs

2 - 4 tablespoons canola oil

Sauté bacon and onion. Add to
venison and sausage. Add jelly,
mustard, beaten egg, salt and
pepper. Mix well and shape into 12
croquettes. Dip each croquette into
beaten egg, then flour, egg again,
and roll in bread crumbs.

Heat oil in fry pan and cook
croquettes until golden brown.

Serves 6

*Tip: Venison sausage can be used instead of the pork; however, the pork
adds lots of flavor.*

Mincemeat Pie

Mincemeat:

4 cups cooked, finely chopped
   venison
8 cups peeled and chopped
   apples
2 cups raisins
2 cups beef suet, finely
   chopped or ground (see tips)
4 cups brown sugar
2 teaspoon salt (optional; not
   necessary with spices)
2 tablespoons cloves
2 tablespoons allspice
2 tablespoons cinnamon
2 tablespoons nutmeg
1 cup molasses
Apple juice

Pie:

1 double-crust pie shell
1 large apple
1 pint mincemeat

Combine all mincemeat ingredients in a non-aluminum Dutch oven. Add enough apple juice to make it moist (but not too wet) and simmer until ingredients are tender and it has thickened.

Place bottom crust in pie plate. Peel and slice apple and place one layer of apples on crust. Sprinkle with a little sugar if apples are tart. Cover apples with 1 pint (2 cups) mincemeat. Place top crust over pie, being sure to seal edges well, and cut several vents in center.

Bake at 450 degrees for 5 minutes, reduce heat to 350 degrees and bake for 30 minutes. Serve warm.

Tips: This is a traditional recipe that has been passed on for several generations. The suet adds flavor, but it can be adjusted or omitted if desired. Mincemeat freezes well.

South Carolina Low Country Shrimp Boil

3 pounds smoked venison
  sausage or kielbasa, cut into
  1-inch pieces
8 medium potatoes, cut into
  2-inch pieces
3 onions, cut into 2-inch pieces
3 ribs celery, cut into 2-inch
  pieces
4 tablespoons Old Bay
  Seasoning (or to taste)
10 - 12 ears corn, halved
5 pounds shrimp, headed
3 - 4 pounds crab legs, optional

Fill a large pot half full of water; bring to a boil over medium-high heat. Cook sausage, potatoes, onions, celery and Old Bay Seasoning for 20 minutes or until potatoes are tender. Add corn, shrimp and crab legs; simmer for 3 - 4 minutes or until shrimp turn pink. Drain and serve immediately on large platters from which guests can serve themselves. Melted butter and seafood sauce compliment the meal.

Serves 10 - 12

Tip: Shrimp have internal thermometers and are done when they turn pink. Overcooking makes shrimp tough and chewy.

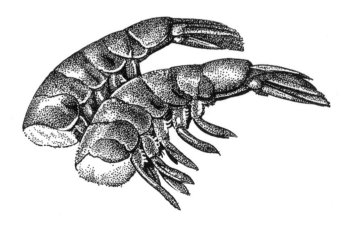

Oven Roasted Ribs

1 deer rib rack

Dry-Spice Rub (what follows is enough for 1 small to medium rack; if your rack is large, double the amount of spice rub):
1 tablespoon chili powder
1 teaspoon ground cumin
1-1/2 teaspoons ground coriander
1-1/2 teaspoons kosher salt
1-1/2 teaspoons paprika
1/2 tablespoon dark brown sugar
1/2 teaspoon black pepper
1/8 teaspoon cayenne pepper (optional)

Stir dry-rub ingredients together in a small bowl. Sprinkle and press rub into both sides of rib rack. Place ribs on broiler-pan rack (spray with Pam and line bottom of pan with foil) meaty side up. Place in a 300-degree oven; rotate pan after first hour and every 30 minutes thereafter until tender (usually about 2 – 2-1/2 hours). If still not tender, continue cooking in 15-minute increments until tender. Brush ribs with your favorite barbecue sauce during the last 10 - 15 minutes of cooking and serve additional sauce for dipping.

Tips: If preferred, you can roast the ribs in the oven and then finish them on a grill with the barbecue sauce. One of our favorite commercial barbecue sauces is Bone Suckin' Sauce. Hunters frequently discard the rib cage, but the meat between the ribs (especially from a young deer) can offer some succulent fare. You have to work to get your dinner, but it is well worthwhile.

Deer Liver Pâté

1 pound deer liver
1 cup milk

1/2 cup unsalted butter, cut
into pieces (divided)
1 tablespoon olive oil
1 cup chopped onion
2 teaspoons minced garlic
2 bay leaves
1/2 teaspoon dried thyme
1/2 teaspoon salt, or to taste
1/2 teaspoon freshly ground
black pepper
1/4 cup brandy

In a bowl, soak the liver in milk for 2 hours. Refrigerate liver while soaking. Drain liver well.

In a large skillet, melt 4 tablespoons butter and 1 tablespoon olive oil over medium-high heat. Add the onions and cook, stirring often, until soft (about 3 minutes). Add the garlic and cook until fragrant (about 30 seconds). Add the liver, bay leaves, thyme, salt and pepper and sauté until the liver is browned on the outside and slightly pink on the inside (about 5 minutes). Remove pan from heat, add brandy, return to heat and flame. Cook until most of the liquid has evaporated and the liver is cooked through but still tender. Remove from heat and cool slightly. Discard bay leaves.

In a food processor, puree the liver mixture. Add the remaining butter in pieces and pulse to blend. Adjust seasonings to taste. Pack the pâté into a mold (sprayed with Pam) and refrigerate until firm (at least 6 hours).

To serve, unmold and garnish with fresh parsley. Surround with baguette croutons, Melba toast, rye toast or toasted pita bread. Gherkin pickles compliment the pâté.

Tip: A little cream can be added when processing if pâté is too thick or stiff.

Fried Deer Liver

1 pound fresh deer liver
1 cup milk

1/4 cup all-purpose flour
1/2 teaspoon salt
1/4 teaspoon black pepper

1 egg, beaten
1/4 cup canola oil, or enough
   to slightly cover bottom of
   pan

Slice liver into thin slices and soak in milk for 2 hours. Drain liver well and pat dry with paper towels.

Dredge liver in seasoned flour, dip in egg and dredge in flour again.

Heat oil over medium-high heat in a large skillet and pan fry liver until golden brown and tender. Serve immediately.

Serves 3 - 4

Tip: If you partially freeze the liver, it is much easier to slice thinly.

Marinated Venison Heart

1 venison heart

Marinade:

1 medium onion, sliced
1 teaspoon prepared mustard
1 teaspoon pickling spices
1 teaspoon salt
1/2 teaspoon whole black
   peppercorns
3 teaspoons wine vinegar
1 cup red wine

Flour
1 tablespoon butter
1 tablespoon olive oil

Split heart in half. Remove all vents and ducts. Rinse well under cool running water. Mix onion, mustard, pickling spices, salt and peppercorns, vinegar and wine in a glass dish; add heart and marinate in refrigerator over night.

Remove heart from marinade, pat dry with paper towels and slice heart thinly.

In a large skillet, melt butter and olive oil over medium-high heat. Dredge heart slices in flour and brown quickly on both sides; reduce heat and cook 5 - 10 minutes longer. Serve immediately.

Chapter 7

Venison Through the Year: Cooking for All Seasons

We tend to associate meals of venison with the hunting season and the long, cold days of winter that follow the rites of autumn. Certainly, a hearty bowl of chili or a bowl of venison stew offers a fine way to eat while hugging the hearth when the weather turns bitter, but the meat is truly one for all seasons. With that in mind, in this chapter we offer a selection of recipes, with a quartet for each season, that celebrates the changes of the year. Let's begin with earth's rebirth and renewal during the greening-up days of spring.

Spring

For those who love the outdoors, the arrival of spring is fraught with meaning. It provides a long-awaited respite from the accumulated miseries, mental and physical, of what old timers often described as cabin fever. On south-facing slopes where the sun first urges sleeping vegetation to awaken, soft, dirty snow gives way to spongy earth awaiting rebirth. Deep down in hardwood sloughs and along field edges wild turkey gobblers announce the dawn of the mating season in ringing, resounding fashion. Wild strawberries bloom in abandoned fields and along paths, offering colorful promise of juicy red jewels that Izaak Walton described in inimitable fashion: "Doubtless God could have made a better berry, but doubtless He never did." Soft rains, followed by a period of clear skies and steady warmth, find morel mushrooms pushing through the cover of leaves where they have been awaiting their few days in the sun. Lettuce and radishes offer the first samplings from gardens, while saxifrage, ramps, poke salad and lamb's quarter provide the perfect spring tonic from the wild. Venison definitely has a place in this time of promise and renewal.

One of the recipes below combines venison with asparagus and green onions, two of the most welcome and most delicious of all spring vegetables. Another uses Vidalia onions, a savory bit of bounty from a section of Georgia that connoisseurs eagerly await every year. Spring is a time for turkey camps and turkey hunters, and what better way to dream and scheme on the eve of opening day than in a hunt-camp bull session where crockpot cubed steak and gravy, perhaps piled atop a fluffy mound of mashed potatoes, fills the inner man.

Venison Loin Steaks with Shrimp and Asparagus Sauce

1 pound venison loin steaks
1/2 pound shrimp
1 pound asparagus
1 package Knorr Bearnaise
    Sauce (or prepare your own
    sauce)
1 tablespoon butter
2 tablespoons olive oil
1/4 cup all-purpose flour
Several green onions

Prepare, cook, peel and chop shrimp and set aside. Prepare and cook asparagus in microwave until tender crisp. Place cooked asparagus in iced water to shock, drain and hold. Prepare bearnaise sauce as directed on the package.

Melt butter and add olive oil in non-stick skillet. Cook green onions, drain and add to bearnaise sauce.

Flatten loin steaks until very thin, lightly flour and brown quickly in remaining drippings in skillet. As steaks brown, add the shrimp and asparagus to the bearnaise sauce to re-heat. Place browned venison loin steaks on platter and top with shrimp and asparagus sauce. Serve immediately.

Tip: Garlic smashed potatoes or oregano roasted potatoes compliment this entree.

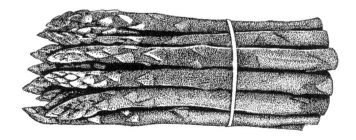

Loin Steaks with Crab Sauce

Steaks:

8 venison loin steaks, 3/4-inch thick
Olive oil
Uncle Buck's Gourmet Steak Seasoning

Sauce:

4 tablespoons butter
3 tablespoons finely chopped sweet onion
1 tablespoon dried parsley
1 tablespoon flour
1 cup fat-free half and half
1/2 cup grated Fontina cheese (Swiss cheese can be used)
1-1/2 teaspoons sherry
1/2 teaspoon salt
1/8 - 1/4 teaspoon black pepper
Dash of red pepper
1/2 pound crab meat

Rub steaks with a drizzle of olive oil and lightly sprinkle with steak seasoning. Marinate for 1 hour. Quickly grill steaks; do not overcook. Steaks should be pink on the inside. Let steaks rest for 5 minutes before topping with crab sauce.

In a heavy sauce pan melt butter and sauté onion. Add parsley and flour, stirring constantly for 1 minute. Add remaining ingredients except crab; stir until cheese melts and sauce is heated through. Gently fold in crab meat. Spoon over steaks.

Serves 8

Tips: For the steaks, an alternative seasoning would be Montreal Steak Seasoning. If you have any crab sauce left, it is delicious in patty shells or over toast. Spring is an especially good time for shellfish.

Greek Venison Wrap

3 slices bacon
1 small Vidalia onion, sliced
   thinly
4 - 5 medium mushrooms,
   sliced thinly
1/2 teaspoon sugar
1 venison loin, sliced thinly
Lemon pepper (to taste) - be
   generous
1 teaspoon lemon juice
2 tortilla wraps, warmed
2 tablespoons sour cream
Fresh spinach leaves
3 - 4 tablespoons feta cheese,
   crumbled

Fry bacon in a skillet until brown; remove from the pan, crumble and set aside. Add onion and mushrooms to pan and sauté until onions are translucent. Add sugar and stir well. Add venison and sprinkle generously with lemon pepper. Add lemon juice and sauté until venison is cooked (but still pink). Warm tortillas in a microwave with a damp paper towel on top. Place sour cream in the center of tortilla, add several leaves of spinach, feta cheese, crumbled bacon and venison mixture. Wrap and serve immediately.

Serves 2

Crockpot Cubed Steak and Gravy

1 pound venison cubed steak
1/2 - 1 cup flour
Salt and pepper to taste
3 - 4 cups water
4 beef bouillon cubes
1 tablespoon Worcestershire
   sauce

Coat steaks with flour, salt and pepper. Place steaks in crockpot. Add remaining flour mixture. Add 3 - 4 cups water, bouillon cubes and Worcestershire sauce. Cook on high setting for 45 minutes; reduce setting to low and cook for 3 - 4 hours. Serve with mashed potatoes, green beans and applesauce for a comforting meal.

Tips: Remember that the bouillon cubes have salt, so adjust your seasoning accordingly. Some cooks prefer to add more Worcestershire sauce (up to 4 tablespoons). If you do not lower the heat, all the gravy will cook away.

Summer

Summertime, and the living is easy. Light meals, outdoor cooking, picnics and an abundance of fresh vegetables mark the season. Two of the recipes that follow emphasize a combination of venison with foods closely associated with summer. One features an interesting and inviting combination of venison and blackberries. Old Will Shakespeare once mused to the effect that if "reasons were only as plentiful as brambles" the world might be quite different. Doubtless there's some depth to the Bard's philosophizing, and no one who knows the backwoods and back roads, who is familiar with the beauty of hidden byways, can doubt his assertions regarding the abundance of brambles (blackberry briars). Picking blackberries means paying some dues in terms of pricked fingers and scratched legs, not to mention sweat equity, but what wonderful eating they make. Whether in a blackberry cobbler, taste-tempting jam liberally applied to a cathead biscuit, fresh atop cereal, with a splashing of cream or enjoyed in some other fashion, these black beauties of the berry world are a delight. Chances are you've never thought about combining them with venison, but try blackberry sauce atop a fine piece of venison and you will experience what Hank Williams, Jr. once described as an "attitude adjustment."

Then there's a different twist when it comes to lasagne. A gardener who can't raise zucchini unquestionably has a green thumb deprivation problem, and as a rule, these members of the squash family produce in such quantities and with so much rapidity that you exhaust all options when it comes to giving them away. Here, zucchini takes the place of pasta, making for a comparatively light and luscious dish.

Add two refreshing salads, both combining venison with a variety of fresh vegetables, and you have a new way to look at summer and some inviting alternatives to the standard summer fare of burgers and barbeque.

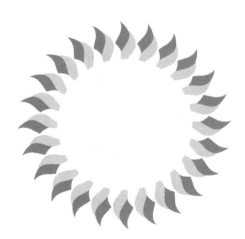

Zucchini Lasagne

4 cups water
6 cups sliced zucchini (about 3
   medium)
2 tablespoons olive oil
1/2 cup chopped onion
1 pound ground venison
2 garlic cloves, minced
2 cups meatless spaghetti sauce
1 teaspoon dried Italian
   seasoning
Cooking spray
2 cups cottage cheese
1 tablespoon dried parsley
2 eggs, lightly beaten
1/2 cup dry bread crumbs,
   divided
2 cups shredded mozzarella
   cheese, divided

Preheat oven to 350 degrees.

Bring water to a boil in a large saucepan. Add zucchini; cook about 3 minutes or until tender crisp. Drain and cool.

Sauté onion in olive oil over medium-high heat until tender. Add ground venison and cook until browned. Add garlic, stirring constantly, and cook about one minute. Stir in spaghetti sauce and Italian seasoning; cook until heated through. Remove from heat.

Combine cottage cheese, parsley and eggs.

Arrange zucchini slices in a 9 x 13-inch pan coated with cooking spray. Sprinkle with half of the bread crumbs. Spread half of the cottage cheese over bread crumbs, cover with half of venison mixture and 1 cup mozzarella cheese. Repeat layers. Reserve remaining cheese.

Bake at 350 degrees for 40 minutes. Sprinkle with remaining mozzarella cheese and bake an additional 5 minutes or until cheese melts.

Serves 8 - 10

Luscious Layered Taco Salad

Dressing:

1/4 cup fresh lime juice
2 tablespoons chopped fresh
  cilantro
1 teaspoon sugar
1/4 teaspoon chili powder
1/8 teaspoon ground cumin
1/4 teaspoon salt
1/8 teaspoon black pepper
1/2 cup extra-virgin olive oil

Venison mixture:

2 tablespoons olive oil
1/2 sweet onion, chopped
2 large garlic cloves, finely
  chopped
1 fresh jalapeño pepper, seeds
  removed and finely chopped
1-1/2 teaspoons chili powder
1 teaspoon ground cumin
1 pound ground venison
1 can (8 ounces) tomato sauce
1 teaspoon kosher salt
1/4 teaspoon freshly ground
  black pepper

Salad:

8 cups fresh lettuce
  (leaf or iceberg)
1 ripe avocado
1 cup grated Mexican cheese
  blend
1 can (15 ounces) black beans,
  drained and rinsed
4 medium tomatoes, chopped
4 ears fresh corn, cooked and
  cut off cob
1 can (6 ounces) sliced pitted
  California black olives,
  drained

To make the dressing, whisk together the lime juice, cilantro, sugar, chili powder, cumin, salt and pepper. Add oil slowly in a stream and whisk until dressing is emulsified.

To make the venison mixture, heat olive oil over medium heat in a heavy skillet. Cook until onion is tender (3 - 5 minutes). Add garlic, jalapeño pepper, chili powder and cumin and sauté about 1 minute, stirring constantly. Add venison and cook, stirring occasionally and breaking up lumps until meat is no longer pink (about 5 minutes). Add tomato sauce, salt and pepper and simmer for 10 - 15 minutes.

To assemble the salad, spread lettuce over bottom of a shallow 4-quart dish (or on 4 individual dinner plates). Spoon venison mixture evenly over lettuce and continue layering with avocado, cheese, black beans, tomatoes,

Luscious Layered Taco Salad *(cont.)*

corn and olives. Drizzle desired amount of dressing over salad.

Serves 4

Tips: The salad is quite different and a tasty way to use ground venison. This is particularly special when fresh tomatoes and corn are available and is a nice way to use any venison remaining in the freezer.

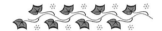

Venison Loin Steaks with Blackberry Sauce

6 - 8 venison loin steaks
Olive oil
Steak seasoning

Sauce:

1-1/2 cups blackberries,
   divided
1/2 cup water
1 tablespoon port wine
2 tablespoons butter
1 tablespoon blackberry jam

Drizzle steaks with olive oil and sprinkle with steak seasoning. Marinate for 30 minutes to 1 hour. Either grill steaks or quickly cook in a non-stick frying pan; do not overcook. Steaks should still be pink in the center.

In a small sauce pan, bring 1 cup blackberries and 1/2 cup water to a boil and reduce heat. Simmer for 30 minutes. Strain berries through a fine sieve. You should have about 1/2 cup sauce. Continue to simmer for about 20 minutes or until sauce is reduced by half (to 1/4 cup). Add port, butter and blackberry jam. Stir constantly until butter melts and blends into sauce. Add remaining 1/2 cup whole berries; stir gently and briefly to heat berries. Serve sauce over steaks.

Tip: Boysenberries or mulberries could be substituted for the blackberries.

Cookout Salad

1 pound ground venison
1 package taco seasoning mix
1/2 cup water
1 head lettuce, shredded
1 green pepper, chopped
1 onion, chopped
2 tomatoes, chopped
1 can (16 ounces) red kidney
   beans, rinsed and drained
1 - 2 cups grated Cheddar
   cheese
12 - 16 ounces tortilla chips,
   crushed
1 bottle Catalina salad dressing

Brown ground venison in a skillet. Add taco seasoning packet and water and simmer until thickened and flavors are blended. Cool slightly. Place remaining ingredients (except dressing) in a large salad bowl, add cooked venison, top with dressing and toss to mix well. Serve immediately.

Tip: Soak chopped onion in iced water for 10 minutes to remove some of the sharpness.

Fall

As the heat and humidity of summer's dog days give way to the first hints of cooler air, the hunter's heart quickens. It's a time for scouting, checking out the progress of food plots, hanging tree stands, shooting bows and sighting guns. Before long, the hunter's moon will turn the evening horizon a lovely orange, and big bucks will move into their pre-rut mode. Many of these activities produce hearty appetites, and it is time to dispose of any venison remaining from the previous year's hunting. One way to use venison comes through combining venison with the doves from September hunts that mark, over much of the country, the return of another hunting season. Bogs go by various names, including pilaus, pilafs and others. The word bog just happens to be the one used in our part of the world to describe any of many savory meat and rice combinations, so it is the one offered here in a venison/dove combination. Then there are chicken-fried venison steaks and two international approaches, one Italian and the other British, to venison cookery. The four recipes use kielbasa, cubed steaks and ground venison, and if you have these left come fall, they provide perfect answers to freezer cleanup.

Deer and Dove Bog

Dove Stock:

**Leftovers after breasting 6
  dozen doves
1 bay leaf
1 teaspoon garlic salt
Dash of red pepper flakes**

Bog:

**1 tablespoon olive oil
1/2 cup onion
1 cup chopped venison
  kielbasa
1 garlic clove, minced
1 cup rice
2 to 2-1/2 cups dove stock
2 cups dove meat
1/2 teaspoon kosher salt
1/2 teaspoon freshly ground
  black pepper**

To prepare stock, place all ingredients in a Dutch oven and cover with cold water. Slowly bring to a simmer, cover and simmer for 2 hours or until meat is tender and falling off the bones.

To prepare bog, place olive oil in a Dutch oven and heat until it shimmers. Add onion and sauté until translucent. Add chopped venison kielbasa, garlic and rice and continue sautéing for 1 minute. Add 2 cups dove stock, bring to a boil, reduce heat and cook for 15 minutes. Add dove meat, salt, pepper and additional 1/2 cup stock if needed and cook 5 more minutes or until rice is tender.

Serves 6

Tips: Since this recipe uses the remainders from filleting dove breasts, it is important to check the meat thoroughly for bones. This makes use of tidbits of dove normally discarded in the cleaning process. You can also, if desired, save dove hearts and use them.

Italian Venison

1/4 cup all-purpose flour
Salt and pepper
1 pound cubed venison steaks,
   or tenderize with a meat
   mallet
2 tablespoons canola oil
1 onion, sliced
2 garlic cloves, minced
1 jar prepared spaghetti sauce
1 teaspoon oregano

Flour and season steaks. Brown steaks in hot oil in a skillet. Place in a casserole dish. If needed, add more oil and sauté onions and garlic. Place on top of steaks. Pour spaghetti sauce over top and sprinkle with oregano. Cover and bake at 350 degrees for 1 hour or until tender. Serve with Caesar salad, garlic spaghetti and freshly grated Parmesan cheese.

Chicken-Fried Steak

1 pound cubed venison steaks
1/4 teaspoon kosher salt
1/4 teaspoon black pepper,
    freshly ground

38 saltine crackers (1 sleeve),
    crushed
1 cup flour
1/2 teaspoon baking powder
1/2 teaspoon black pepper,
    freshly ground
Several dashes ground red
    pepper

2 large eggs
3/4 cup milk

6 - 8 tablespoons canola oil

4 tablespoons flour
2 cups milk

Chopped parsley for garnish

Sprinkle salt and pepper on both sides of steaks and set aside.

Combine cracker crumbs, 1 cup flour, baking powder, black and red peppers.

Whisk together 3/4 cup milk and 2 eggs. Dredge steaks in cracker-crumb mixture, dip in milk/egg mixture, and dredge in cracker mixture again. Push steaks into crumbs to cover well.

Pour oil into a large cast iron skillet and heat. Have oil hot and fry steaks quickly. Turn only once and brown on each side. Keep steaks warm in a 225-degree oven.

Leave 4 tablespoons oil (and browned bits) in pan. Add 4 tablespoons flour and cook about 1 minute until slightly brown. Remove from heat and add 2 cups milk, stirring constantly. Return to medium heat and stir constantly until thickened.

Serve gravy with steaks and mashed potatoes. Sprinkle with parsley, if desired.

Tips: Serve with garlic green beans and hot biscuits. Leftovers make good sandwiches. Fudgy Texas cake tops off this meal.

Quick and Easy Shepherd's Pie

1 tablespoon olive oil
1/2 - 3/4 pound ground
    venison
1 package (1.2 ounces) gravy
    mix (Knorr Hunter
    Mushroom and Gravy Mix)
1/4 teaspoon black pepper
1 package (10 ounces) frozen
    peas, thawed
1/2 cup carrots (frozen or
    canned), cooked
1/2 cup canned pearl onions,
    drained
1 package (20 ounces)
    prepared mashed potatoes
    (such as Simply Potatoes)
1/2 cup Romano cheese

Preheat oven to 350 degrees.

In a large, non-stick skillet, cook ground venison until it is no longer pink. Add the gravy mix, black pepper and 1 cup water. Stir constantly until the sauce comes to a boil; cook for 1 minute. Spray a deep-dish pie plate or 9-inch-square baking dish with vegetable cooking spray. Spoon in the meat. Top with peas, carrots and onions. Spread mashed potatoes evenly over vegetables. Sprinkle with cheese. Bake 25-30 minutes or until heated through and the top is golden brown.

Serves 4 - 5

Tips: Fresh onion can be cooked with the venison if you prefer. Green beans can be substituted for the green peas. Corn can be added if desired.

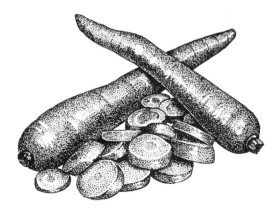

Winter

Another hunting season, hopefully filled with the sort of success that fills the freezer and sustains the sportsman, has come and gone. It is time to look back on the rites of autumn with reflective longing, and there are few better ways to do so than while preparing or eating a meal built around a main dish featuring venison. Here are four dishes as hearty, tasty and fulfilling as anyone could want. Discerning readers might well notice that three of the four recipes feature the names of individuals. That is because the recipes come from friends and family, and what better time to celebrate the sort of camaraderie and togetherness afforded by deer hunting than through shared recipes? These four offerings vary appreciably, but all share a common virtue. They promise to stoke the inner fires against even the most bitter of cold even while evoking fond reminiscence of hunts past, whether it is the one that produced the meal being enjoyed or a day afield stretching far back along a darkening road into the dim and distant past.

Gail's Spicy Mustard Fried Venison

4 pounds venison cubed steak

16 ounces yellow mustard

1/4 cup Worcestershire sauce

1 tablespoon Tony Chachere's Creole Seasoning (or to taste)

Several shakes Texas Pete Hot Sauce (or to taste)

1 cup flour

Salt to taste

Canola or vegetable oil to cover bottom of frying pan

Mix mustard, Worcestershire sauce, creole seasoning and hot sauce in a large bowl. Add steaks in batches and toss to cover well. Place flour and salt in a gallon resealable plastic bag, add venison and shake well.

Preheat canola oil in a large frying pan and quickly brown steaks on both sides. Do not overcook; steaks should be golden brown but pink in the center.

Serves 12

Steak and Potatoes

1 pound venison cubed steak

2 tablespoons olive oil

1 can (10.75 ounces) cream of celery soup

1/2 cup milk

1/2 cup sour cream

1/4 teaspoon freshly ground black pepper

16 ounces frozen hash browns, thawed (cubed style)

1/2 cup shredded Cheddar cheese

1 can (3 ounces) French fried onions

Brown venison steaks in olive oil in a skillet and set aside. Combine soup, milk, sour cream and pepper. Stir in thawed potatoes, 1/3 cup cheese, and 1/2 can onions. Spoon mixture into 9 x 13-inch baking dish. Arrange steaks over potatoes. Bake covered, at 350 degrees for 45 - 50 minutes. Top with remaining cheese and onions and bake, uncovered, 5 - 10 minutes longer.

Eric's Goulash

2 tablespoons olive oil
1/2 stick butter
1 large onion, chopped
1/2 green pepper, chopped
1-1/2 to 2 pounds venison stew
   meat
2 cans (14 ounces each) stewed
   tomatoes
1 can (14 ounces) diced
   tomatoes
1 can (6 ounces) tomato paste
1/2 cup sun-dried tomatoes
1/2 teaspoon salt
1/2 teaspoon black pepper
2 - 3 teaspoons Hungarian
   paprika
1 bay leaf
1 teaspoon Worcestershire
   sauce

Sauté onion and pepper in olive oil and butter mixture; add venison and brown. Add all other ingredients and simmer for 1 - 2 hours or until thickened. Adjust seasoning if needed. Serve over wide noodles or dumplings.

Tip: This is actually better the second day because the flavors blend.

Upgren Venison Stroganoff

2 pounds venison steak, cut
   1/2-inch thick

2 cups chopped mushrooms

1 cup finely chopped onion

1/4 cup butter or shortening

3 beef bouillon cubes

1 cup boiling water

2 tablespoons tomato paste

1 teaspoon dry mustard

1/2 teaspoon salt

2 tablespoons flour

1/2 cup water

1 cup sour cream

4 cups cooked rice

Cut steak into strips 2-1/4 inches long. In a large skillet, sauté fresh mushrooms and onion in 3 tablespoons butter until golden brown; remove from the pan. Brown meat on all sides. Dissolve bouillon cubes in water; pour over meat. Add tomato paste, mustard and salt. Bring to a boil, reduce heat and simmer for 45 minutes or until meat is tender. Combine flour and water. Slowly stir into meat mixture. Cook, stirring constantly, until the mixture comes to a boil; reduce heat. Add mushrooms, onions and sour cream. Heat through but do not boil. Serve over hot rice or chow mein noodles.

Serves 4 - 6

Menus

Spicy Tomato Juice Cocktail
Loin Steaks with Crab, Shrimp and Scallop Sauce*
Garlic Spaghetti
Strawberry Spinach Salad
Hot Crunchy Rolls
Ice Cream Pie with Black Walnut Crust
White Zinfandel Wine or Hazelnut Cream Coffee

Cranberry Meatballs*
Cook Out Time Burgers and Hot Dogs*
Chili Sauce for Burgers or Hot Dogs*
Onion Rolls and Buns
Venison Sausage Baked Beans*
Cole Slaw
Assorted Pickles, Relishes and Chips
Strawberry Trifle
Lemonade or Iced Beer

Venison Loin Steaks with Shrimp and Asparagus Sauce*
Garlic Smashed Potatoes
Mixed Greens with Black Walnut Vinaigrette
Crusty Sour Dough Bread
Double Chocolate Brownies
Chablis Wine or Columbian Supreme Coffee

Pasta E Fagoli*
Hunter's Green Salad and Dressing
Freshly Baked Garlic Bread Sticks
Lemon Chess Pie
Chianti Wine or Summertime Tea

Crockpot Onion and Game Stew*
Spinach and Avocado Salad
Hot Herb Bread
Baked Pears topped with Chocolate Sauce
Tea or Coffee

Quick and Simple Chili*
Assorted Crackers and Saltines
Chocolate-Dipped Nuts, Mixed
    Fresh Fruits and Cheese Platter
Frosty Mugs of Beer or Cider

*Salisbury Steak with Mushroom
    Wine Gravy**
Oven Baked Brown Rice with Wild
    Mushrooms
Watercress Salad with Parmesan
    Mustard Dressing
Homemade Garden Herb Bread
Vanilla Ice Cream with Raspberry
    Sauce
Merlot Wine or Beer

Loin Steaks with Mango Salsa*
Wild Rice
Green Beans, Onions, and Toasted
    Walnut Salad
Homemade Cracked Wheat Bread
Grilled Pineapple over Rum Raisin
    Ice Cream
Raspberry Tea or Coffee

*Venison Loin Steaks with Shrimp
    Gravy**
Garlic Cheese Grits*
Creamy Green Pea Salad
Fresh Blueberry Pie and Ice Cream
Liebfraumilch Wine or French Roast
    Coffee

Easy Pizza Venison Swiss Steak*
Poppy Seed Noodles
Wilted Spinach Salad
Texas Garlic Toast
Lime Sherbert and Sugar Cookies
Lemon Tea or Amaretto Coffee

Lima Bean Chowder*
Grilled Cheese Sandwiches
Pear and Hazelnut Salad
Chocolate Chip Cookies
Coffee or Tea

Luscious Layered Taco Salad*
Baked Spicy Tortilla Triangles
Iced Cold Watermelon Wedges
Homemade Cinnamon Ice Cream
Corona with Lime or Lemonade

*recipe included in cookbook

Appendix

Sources of Useful Supplies

SPICES AND HERBS

When it comes to spices, herbs and seasonings, the best are those you can grow in your own garden. These have a freshness, taste and pungency unmatched by anything you can buy. Our family garden features a wide assortment of herbs, and the capability of walking out into the backyard to snip some chives or cut some fresh oregano brings us considerable pleasure. However, even if you are a keen gardener, unless you are among the fortunate few who have a greenhouse, at times you will have to rely on what my grandfather used to call "store-bought stuff." Here are some connections we have found useful, and of course, those connected to the Internet can use search engines to find many more.

Penzey's Spices, P. O. Box 924, Brookfield, WI 53008-0924
Toll-free orders: 1-800-741-7787
www.penzeys.com

Lawry's Foods Inc., 22 E. Huntington Drive, Monrovia, CA 91016-3500
Telephone: 626-930-8816
www.lawrys.com

Spices etc. . . . , P. O. Box 2088, Savannah, GA 31402-2088
Toll-free orders: 1-800-827-6373
www.spicesetc.com

The Sausage Maker, Inc., 1500 Clinton Street, Bldg. 123, Buffalo, NY 14206
Toll-free Orders: 1-800-490-8525
www.sausagemaker.com

All American Spices (handle all McCormick brands of spices and herbs)
Telephone: 617-698-4928
www.aaspices.com

Eastman Outdoors, Inc., P. O. Box 380, Flushing, MI 48433
Toll-free orders: 1-800-241-4833
www.eastmanoutdoors.com

Coyote Country Seasoning Company
Toll-free orders: 1-800-852-7454
www.coyotecountry.com

SAUSAGE MAKING, JERKY

Eldon's Jerky and Sausage Supply, HC75, Box 113 A2, Kooskia, ID
83539
Toll-free orders: 1-800-352-9453
www.eldonssausage.com

Butcher & Packer Supply Company, 1468 Gratiot Avenue, Detroit,
MI 48207
Toll-free orders: 1-800-521-3188
www.butcher-packer.com

LEM Products, Inc., 107 May Drive, Harrison, OH 45030
Toll-free orders: 1-877-536-7763
www.lemproducts.com

SAWS, KNIVES, OTHER PROCESSING TOOLS AND SHARPENERS

While the direct contact information is provided here, most of these
hunter-handy items are available through local retail stores and
catalog sales.

Buck Knives, Inc., P. O. Box 1267, El Cajon, CA 92022
Telephone 619-449-1100
www.buckknives.com

Camp Chef, P. O. Box 4057, Logan, UT 84323
Toll-free orders: 1-800-650-2433
www.campchef.com

Diamond Machining Technology, Inc., Hayes Memorial Drive,
Marlborough, MA 01752
Telephone 1-800-6664368
www.dmt-sharp.com

Gatco Sharpeners, P. O. Box 600, Getzville, NY 14068-0600
Telephone 716-877-2200
www.greatamericantoolcompany.com

Gerber Legendary Blades, 14200 S.W. 72nd Ave., Portland, OR 97223
Toll-free: 1-800-950-6161
www.gerberblades.com

Lansky Sharpeners, P. O. Box 800, Buffalo, NY 14231-0880
Telephone: 716-877-7511
www.lansky.com

Remington Arms Company
870 Remington Drive, P.O. Box 700, Madison, NC 27025-0700
Telephone: 1-800-243-9700
www.remington.com

Schrade Cutlery
Imperial Schrade Corporation, 7 Schrade
Court, Ellenville, NY 12428
Telephone: 845-647-7600
www.schradeknives.com